DEAR RETAIL,

GRILL

HAPPILY!

LOVE,

ME

(AMANDA

MARGARETE)

How To Plan A Safe Party & Why It Is So Important

Party the safe way

The basic ingredients of a good cookout haven't changed much over the years. Delicious food, enjoyable guests, tasty beverages and plenty of fun are all essential parts of the recipe for a successful gathering of friends, relatives or business associates.

But lately, caring hosts and hostesses have added another important element — safety. Most people realize they have a responsibility to protect their guests from the dangers of drinking and driving.

In fact, in many states, social hosts can be held legally and financially liable for serving alcohol to minors or adult guests who are intoxicated and then cause crashes that result in fatalities or serious injuries.

Food Writers' Favorites/Quick & Easy Recipes: Grilling is the third volume in our "Safe Party Planning" cookbook series. Serving a wide variety of delicious grilled food is just one way to increase the likelihood that your guests will not attempt to drive home under the influence of alcohol.

You can make your next party, picnic or business meeting a memorable and safe occasion for everyone by adopting the following strategies.

Plan responsibly

Here are a few tips you can follow — before the party even starts:

1

- Invite guests who are compatible. People who feel left out of the action at a party may have a tendency to drink too much.

- Plan lots of group activities, games or sports. Keep your guests occupied, so that they spend more time participating in activities other than excessive drinking.

- Be honest. If you're inviting guests who sometimes drink to excess, tell them that you will not permit them to drive home under the influence of alcohol.

Select a Designated Driver

The Designated Driver is an important guest at any party — because he or she volunteers to provide a safe and sober ride home for anyone who needs it.

It's easy to be a Designated Driver. All it takes is a promise not to drink any alcohol before or during the outing.

As your guests arrive, ask if they've made arrangements for a safe and sober ride home. If not, help them pick someone in their group to be the Designated Driver for the party. If no one is willing inform them of the availability of the person you have designated. You can even volunteer to be a Designated Driver, if necessary.

Treat all the Designated Drivers with respect. They are doing you a favor by helping your guests arrive at their homes safe and sober.

Be a responsible host

Mingle with your guests during the party. Take a few moments to chat with everyone you've invited. It's a good way to show your guests that you're happy to see them — and to notice if anyone should stop drinking alcohol.

- Make food — instead of drink — the focus of attention. Set up a buffet. Let your guests create their own dishes with an array of appetizers, salads and entrées. Chocolates, pastries and other goodies are a great way to divert people away from alcoholic beverages.

- Limit the amount of salty snacks you serve. Salted chips, pretzels, nuts and other highly salted foods can build up a thirst and lead guests to drink more alcohol.

- Prepare a variety of nonalcoholic beverages and encourage your guests to try them. Let them know that you'll share your recipes the next time they have a party or leave recipe cards on the table.

- Don't let guests serve themselves alcohol. Use a responsible bartender or prepare all alcoholic drinks yourself. Stick to exact measurements for all mixed drinks. Never serve alcohol to any guest who is under 21 years old or who has had too much to drink.

- Close the bar early. Stop serving alcohol at least 90 minutes before the end of the party. Offer your guests coffee, tea and other nonalcoholic beverages instead.

Greet every guest as they prepare to leave

As your guests prepare to leave, tell them not to drive if you think they have had too much to drink. Call a cab, drive them home yourself or invite them to stay at your place until they're completely sober the next day. Never let anyone drive while under the influence of alcohol.

Start planning your next party now

Invite a few friends and relatives over to sample the recipes in this book. We think you and your guests will agree that this collection of grilled foods offers something to satisfy every taste.

But before the fun starts, please take a few moments to read the rest of this chapter.

The following pages will help you learn more about MADD's goals and programs — and why your support will help us put an end to drinking and driving. Thank you.

Mothers Against Drunk Driving

We're still MADD

Mothers Against Drunk Driving was founded in 1980 after a California woman's daughter was killed by a hit-and-run driver. Incredibly, the driver had been released from jail on bail just two days earlier — for another drunk driving hit-and-run crime.

Determined to stop the tragic loss of life caused by drinking and driving, the girl's mother and others in her community formed the first chapter of MADD.

Today, that one small group of committed women has grown to a nationwide grass-roots movement with more than 500 community action teams, chapters and state organizations across the United States.

And MADD is not just for mothers. Our approximately 3.2 million members and supporters include fathers, sons, brothers, grandparents and uncles. In fact, anyone can join MADD. The only requirement is a commitment to end alcohol- and other drug-impaired driving.

Since MADD began, more than 2,000 anti-drunk driving laws have been passed nationwide. These laws are helping police, prosecutors and judges remove impaired drivers from our highways — and keep them off.

But laws alone can't stop people from drinking and driving.

MADD is educating the public about the dangers of impaired driving. Through programs like Designated Driver and Project Red Ribbon, we're spreading this important message across America — drinking and driving must stop.

After more than a decade of battling drinking and driving, we're still MADD. And we're still committed to ending the senseless injuries and deaths caused by drunk driving.

You can help MADD
MADD needs your help — because drinking and driving affects everyone.

Along with the human toll in destroyed lives, drunk driving costs the United States $44 billion every year in direct expenses. An additional $90 billion is lost in quality of life due to these crashes.

As a team, MADD and you are working to keep drunk drivers off our highways. Here are a few ways you can make a difference:

• Make a personal promise to never drink and drive.

• Don't let friends or relatives drive under the influence of alcohol or other drugs.

• Speak out in your community against alcohol- and other drug-impaired driving.

• Support tougher legislation against drunk driving. Tell your local, county, state, and federal representatives that their help is needed to end drinking and driving.

• Use a Designated Driver if you drink when you're out. Encourage friends and relatives to use and to be Designated Drivers.

• Warn the young people in your life about the dangers of under-age drinking and impaired driving.

• Never serve alcohol to anyone under 21 years old or anyone who has had too much to drink.

• Report drunk drivers to the police.

• Remember that a person's ability to drive can be greatly affected by alcohol long before he or she appears to be intoxicated.

Your help makes a difference
Thanks to the help of millions of concerned and committed people across America, alcohol-related traffic deaths have decreased approximately 38 percent since MADD was founded in 1980.

But there's so much more hard work ahead of us.

Two out of every five Americans will be involved in an alcohol- or other drug-related crash during their lives. We want to reduce those odds—and protect you from the threat of drinking and driving.

In 1993, an estimated 17,461 people died and 950,000 people were injured as the result of alcohol-related crashes on the nation's highways.

Each death and injury is a solemn reminder that MADD must continue the battle against drinking and driving. And we will continue to do everything possible to make our roads safer — for everyone.

MADD's goals

In 1990, MADD released its "20 By 2000" plan – to reduce the proportion of traffic fatalities which were alcohol-related from 50% to 40% by the year 2000. Since that time this proportion dropped from 50% to 43.5%. We have surpassed the half-way mark, but there's still much to do. The "20 By 2000" plan includes:

- *Youth Issues*
  Education, prevention and penalties for alcohol and other drug use by those under age 21, whether driving or not.

- *Enforcement*
  Sobriety checkpoints, a .08 blood alcohol content limit and mandatory testing of drivers involved in fatal and serious injury crashes.

- *Sanctions*
  Administrative license revocation, plate or vehicle confiscation for repeat offenders and equal penalties for death and serious injury DUI/DWI offenses.

- *Self-Sufficiency*
  DUI/DWI fines, fees, and other assessments to fund programs to prevent, detect and deter impaired driving.

- *Responsible Marketing & Service of Alcohol*
  Uniform closing hours for drinking establishments, Designated Driver programs, server training and an end to happy hours.

- *Amendments for Victims Rights*
  State constitutional amendments to ensure that victims will be informed of, present at and heard in the criminal justice process.

- *Compensation for Victims*
  Restitution and victim compensation programs to assure adequate financial recovery for victims.

- *Dram Shop Recovery*
  Legislation or case law to allow victims the right to seek financial recovery from servers who provided alcohol to those who are intoxicated or to minors who then cause fatal or serious injury crashes.

- *Endangerment of Children*
  Legislation to enhance the sanctions of convicted impaired drivers who drove with a minor child in the vehicle.

MADD is on your side

Mothers Against Drunk Driving is more committed than ever to protecting you, your family and your friends from the threat of alcohol- and other drug-related driving crashes.

But we want you to know that MADD is only a phone call away if you or anyone you know is ever the victim of a drunk driving crash.

Call our hot line at 1-800-GET-MADD. Our trained staff is prepared to give victims immediate emotional support and advice on the criminal justice system. And we'll direct victims to the MADD chapter nearest them, so that they can receive personalized support and understanding they need.

MADD can help stop the alcohol- and other drug-related crashes that destroy so many lives each year. Please, help us in whatever way you can to make our highways safer. Thank you.

If you would like more information on MADD in your local community or how to get more involved, write: MADD National Office, 511 E. John Carpenter Freeway, Suite 700, Irving, TX 75062 *or call:* 1-800-GET-MADD

Food Writer's Favorites Series
Food Editor's Hometown Favorites
Food Editor's Favorites Treasured Recipes
Food Editor's Favorites Desserts
Food Writer's Favorites Soups, Stews and Casseroles
Food Writer's Favorites Cookies
Food Writer's Favorites Salads
Food Writer's Favorites Safe Party Planning: Beverages
Food Writer's Favorites Quick & Easy Recipes: Entrées
Food Writer's Favorites Safe Party Planning, Vol. 2
     Quick & Easy Recipes: Appetizers

QUICK & EASY RECIPES

GRILLING

FOOD WRITERS' FAVORITES

EDITED BY BARBARA GIBBS OSTMANN AND JANE BAKER

About the Editors

Jane Baker is marketing director for the Cherry Marketing Institute in Michigan. She was food editor of *The Phoenix* (Ariz.) *Gazette* for 14 years. Jane uses her expertise as a home economist and writer to pursue free-lance writing and editing opportunities.

Barbara Gibbs Ostmann writes about food and travel for The New York Times Regional Newspaper Group and other publications. She was food editor of the *St. Louis* (Mo.) *Post-Dispatch* for 16 years prior to becoming an assistant professor and the coordinator of the Agricultural Journalism program at the University of Missouri-Columbia.

Contributing Writers

Jane Baker, East Lansing, MI; **Laura Barton**, Portland, OR; **Gail Bellamy**, *Restaurant Hospitality*, Cleveland, OH; **Barbara Burklo**, (Retired) *Santa Cruz Sentinel*, Soquel, CA; **Toni Burks**, Roanoke, VA; **Narcisse S. Cadgène**, New York, NY; **Debra Carr-Elsing**, *The Capital Times*, Madison, WI; **Dorothy Cunningham**, Morenci, MI; **Louise Dodd**, *Courier Herald*, Dublin, GA; **Beth Whitley Duke**, *Amarillo Globe-News*, Amarillo, TX; **Clara H. Eschmann**, *The Macon Telegraph*, Macon, GA; **Barbara Fisher**, *This Week Publications*, Farmingdale, NY; **Carolyn Flournoy**, *The Times*, Shreveport, LA; **Paula M. Galusha**, Tulsa, OK; **Janet Geissler**, *Lansing State Journal*, Lansing, MI; **Jane Gray**, *Ludington Daily News*, Ludington, MI; **Teri M. Grimes**, *The Bradenton Herald*, Bradenton, FL; **Lorrie Guttman**, *Tallahassee Democrat*, Tallahassee, FL; **Suzanne Hall**, *The Chattanooga Times*, Chattanooga, TN; **Alice Handkins**, Wichita, KS; **Zack Hanle**, *Bon Appétit*, New York, NY; **Constance Hay**, Coumbia, MD; **Jim Hillibish**, *The Repository*, Canton, OH; **Mary Beth Jung**, Grafton, WI; **Susan Manlin Katzman**, St. Louis, MO; **Sue Kurth**, *Beloit Daily News*, Beloit, WI; **Stacy Lam**, *The Macon Telegraph*, Macon, GA; **Beth W. Orenstein**, Northampton, PA; **Eleanor Ostman**, *St. Paul Pioneer Press*, St. Paul, MN; **Barbara Gibbs Ostmann**, St. Louis, MO; **Christine Randall**, *The Post and Courier*, Charleston, SC; **Marion Riedl**, *Ludington Daily News*, Ludington, MI; **Nancy Ross Ryan**, *Restaurants & Institutions*, Des Plaines, IL; **Sally Scherer**, *The Macon Telegraph*, Macon, GA; **Mary D. Scourtes**, *The Tampa Tribune*, Tampa, FL; **Caroline Stuart**, Greenwich, CT; **Jeanne Voltz**, Pittsboro, NC; **Ann Corell Wells**, *The Grand Rapids Press*, Grand Rapids, MI; **Kasey Wilson**, *The Vancouver Courier*, Vancouver, BC, Canada; **Barbara Yost**, *The Phoenix Gazette*, Phoenix, AZ.

CONTENTS

1   How To Plan A Safe Party & Why It Is So Important

4   Information About MADD

12   Grilling

13   Grilling Guidelines

17   Meats

47   Poultry

69   Fish & Seafood

91   Vegetables & Fruits

115   Sauces & Marinades

135   Accompaniments

GRILLING

Americans have taken the art of grilling foods, first enjoyed by our ancestors more than 100,000 years ago, to new dimensions. Smart outdoor cooks have learned to grill almost everything to perfection — from whole turkeys and chickens to fish and seafood, from appetizers to side dishes. Many backyard chefs grill all year round, and even people who'd never dream of cooking in a regular kitchen will gladly take a turn at the barbecue grill.

Outdoor grilling is an easy way to entertain and great fun for the host and hostess, as well as guests. You can grill at the beach or in the mountains or right in your own backyard, after work or on weekends.

This collection of easy recipes is bursting with hot new ideas for outdoor dining. Food editors and writers from across the country have shared their tried-and-true personal favorites, as well as many regional specialties. In addition to favorite recipes for the grill, there is a special section on accompaniments — potato salad, baked beans, cole slaw and much more — all perfect to serve with grilled foods.

On the following pages are tips on how to make outdoor cooking even easier and more fun. In addition, each recipe in the book includes a brief introduction that tells you something about the recipe and may offer grilling tips.

We would like to make it clear that these recipes are the contributors' favorites. The publisher makes no claim that the recipes are original. When possible, credit has been given where credit is due.

We hope the recipes in this book will entice you and your family to fire up the grill and get cookin'!

Jane Baker and Barbara Gibbs Ostmann
Editors of *Food Writers' Favorites*
Quick & Easy Recipes: Grilling

GRILLING GUIDELINES

Grilling is a fun and easy cookery method, but even experienced grill cooks may find these how-to suggestions helpful.

Getting Started

- There are many kinds of grills on the market, from simple braziers and hibachis to kettle-shaped charcoal grills and elaborate gas and electric models that rival the ranges in most kitchens. Choose the grill that best suits your needs.
- One factor to consider when purchasing a grill is whether the grill is covered or not. Some foods, such as a roast turkey or slow-cooking barbecues, require a covered grill.
- The recipes in this book are designed for outdoor cooking. However, most of the recipes can be adapted for use on an indoor grill or oven broiler, if desired.
- If you are using a charcoal grill, wait until white ash has formed on the coals (usually 40 to 45 minutes after lighting the briquets), then spread out the coals before you begin cooking.
- Preheating a gas or electric grill (usually only 5 to 10 minutes) is helpful. Follow manufacturer's instructions.
- To reduce flare-ups and to lower the temperature of a charcoal grill, raise the grill rack (if possible), spread coals apart or open the vents (if using a covered grill).
- To increase the temperature, tap ashes off with tongs, move coals closer together, add briquets, lower the grill rack or close the vents halfway (if using a covered grill).
- To lower or increase the heat on a gas or electric grill, just turn the temperature controls.

How Hot Is Hot

- Cooking times vary widely when grilling. Wind, temperature, the size of the food and whether the grill is covered or not all affect cooking time.
- Recipes in this cookbook give approximate cooking times and tests for doneness, if appropriate. Use this information as a guide to determine when the food is cooked properly. Some foods may need to cook longer; others may be done in a shorter amount of time. Most grill cooks will tell you that experience is the best teacher.
- If your grill does not have a temperature gauge, you can use a hand test to determine approximate temperature. Carefully hold your hand, palm-side down, about 4 inches above the coals. Count the seconds you can keep your hand in place before the heat becomes uncomfortable:

    2 seconds — a hot fire, 375° or more.
    3 seconds — a medium-hot fire, 350° to 375°.
    4 seconds — a medium fire, 300° to 350°.
    5 seconds — a low fire, 200° to 300°.

Safety Savvy

- Be sure the grill is on a solid, heat-proof surface in an open, well-ventilated area.
- Keep the grill away from shrubbery, grass, buildings or overhangs. Don't grill in the garage, even with the door open. Likewise, don't grill under a covered patio.
- Never use kerosene or gasoline to start a fire.
- Never leave a lighted grill unattended.
- Keep children (and pets) away from a lighted grill. If older children want to learn how to grill, teach them safe grilling techniques first.
- Never add charcoal briquets that have been doused with starter fluid to a fire that is already burning. If you need to add additional charcoal during the cooking process, add plain briquets to the fire, one at a time, using long-handled tongs.

- Remember that the coals, grill, rack and tools are hot. Use flame-resistant hot pads or mitts when cooking and handling the grill and tools.
- Keep a spray bottle filled with water nearby to stop flare-ups on charcoal grills. For gas and electric grills, reduce the temperature.
- Practice food safety guidelines from the time the food is purchased and prepped in the kitchen. Cross-contamination from plates, utensils or sauces is a serious health risk.
- During the marinating process, the marinade can become contaminated with microorganisms from the raw meat, fish or poultry. Any marinade or basting sauce that has touched raw meat (blood) must be properly heated before serving it alongside the grilled food. Bring the sauce or marinade to a full boil, then simmer it 5 to 10 minutes before serving. Discard any leftover sauce. To eliminate the need for this procedure, the sauce can be separated into two portions: one portion for marinating/basting and the other for serving with the cooked meat.

Adding Fragrant Flavors
- Grilled foods take on new flavors when hardwood chips, herbs or other seasonings are added to the fire.
- Hickory wood chips add an intense, sweet flavor to grilled foods and are especially good with pork, ham and beef.
- Mesquite chips or mesquite charcoal briquets are especially popular for grilling beef. Mesquite gives foods a light, sweet, smoky flavor.
- Apple and cherry wood chips give a mild, sweet flavor that is especially good with poultry and game hens.
- Alder is delicate and fragrant, perfect for salmon or other fish.
- When using wood chips, soak them in enough water to cover for 30 to 60 minutes, then drain. Sprinkle chips over hot coals. Add more chips every 15 to 20 minutes.
- Use only wood from fruit or nut trees. Soft woods or evergreen woods, such as pine, should not be used because their resins discolor the food and give it a bitter taste.

- Grapevine cuttings add a sweet, wine-like flavor to foods and are especially good with fish and poultry. Just toss the dry vines onto the fire. They produce a quick burst of heat, then smoke lightly.
- The branches of various herb plants, such as thyme, rosemary, sage and oregano, can be used to add flavor to grilled foods. Soak branches in water, shake off excess water, then add branches to hot coals, a few at a time. Or place the soaked and drained branches on the cooking rack along with the food, instead of on the coals.
- Cinnamon sticks, garlic cloves, citrus peels and whole nutmegs are some of the spices that can be used for flavoring grilled foods. Soak whole spices in water before adding to the coals; they should smolder and smoke, not burn to a crisp.

Quick Clean-Up

- Easy clean-up begins BEFORE you start grilling. Coat the grill rack with nonstick cooking spray before you place it over the fire.
- Clean the grill as soon as possible after using it. Soak the rack in hot sudsy water in a sink or laundry tub. Scrub it with a stiff grill brush to remove any stubborn spots, then rinse it well with hot water.
- If you do not have a sink or tub large enough to hold the grill rack, cover it with wet paper towels and let it stand at least one hour. This will help to loosen any burned-on food. Remove the paper towels and wash and rinse as directed.

Meats

18	Beef Fajitas
19	Boating Pork Chops
20	Flank Steak Appetizer
21	Foiled Franks
22	Garlic Steak Sandwiches
23	Great Balls of Fire
24	Grilled Ham
25	Grilled Lamb Kebabs
26	Grilled Leg of Lamb
27	Ham Burgers
28	Hot Dogs — Your Way
30	Kiwi Venison Steaks
31	Lamb Steaks Supreme
32	Lemon-Herb Rabbit
33	Manhattan Steak
34	Midwest-Style Spareribs
35	Okie Dokie Barbecued Bologna
36	Plum Delicious Ribs
37	Reubenburgers
38	Seasoned Steak with Grilled Peppers
39	Sour Cream Beef Burgers
40	South African Safari Kebabs
41	Spiedini Sandwiches
42	St. Louis Pork Steaks
43	Texas-Style Ribs
44	The Perfect Burger
45	Tulsa Kebabs
46	Zesty Flank Steak

Beef Fajitas

Carolyn Flournoy
Food Columnist, *The Times*, Shreveport, LA

Because Shreveport is less than 20 miles from the Texas border, our four children grew up eating Tex-Mex food: tamales, enchiladas and their favorite, fajitas, which means "little girdles" and refers to the cut of meat, skirt steak. Because skirt steak used to be quite inexpensive, fajitas also were a hit with my food budget. Fajitas cook on the grill in a matter of minutes, so they make a great last-minute dinner. The marinade is my version of one I learned years ago from a friend in Austin. The go-alongs can vary according to what's in your refrigerator.

Makes 4 servings

1/2 cup vegetable oil	Warm flour tortillas
2 tablespoons lime juice	Sour cream
1 tablespoon Worcestershire sauce	Tomato salsa or picante sauce
1/2 teaspoon granulated sugar	Guacamole
1 teaspoon crushed red pepper	Sliced onions
2 cloves garlic, minced	Sliced green bell peppers
1 small onion, thinly sliced	
1 1/4 pounds beef skirt steak (or beef flank steak)	

In a shallow dish, combine oil, lime juice, Worcestershire sauce, sugar, red pepper flakes, garlic and onion; mix well. Put skirt steak in marinade. Refrigerate, covered, 1 hour, turning occasionally.

When ready to grill, remove meat from marinade; discard marinade. Slice meat into two or three 6-inch pieces.

Place meat on gas grill over medium-high heat or on charcoal grill 4 to 6 inches from medium-hot coals. Cook 3 to 4 minutes per side, turning once, or until done as desired. Cut grilled meat on the diagonal into thin strips.

Roll meat strips in warm flour tortillas. Let diners select their own toppings from sour cream, salsa, guacamole, onions and/or green peppers.

Please don't drink and drive.

Boating Pork Chops

Ann Corell Wells
Food Editor, *The Grand Rapids Press*, Grand Rapids, MI

Sailing friends created this recipe many years ago, because the frozen chops could be taken to the sailboat in a cooler and didn't take up precious space in the boat's tiny refrigerator. I always keep a bag of these marinated chops in the freezer because they make a quick meal. The chops can be grilled frozen when there's no time to thaw them or you can quickly thaw them in the microwave oven.

Makes 4 to 6 servings

4 to 6 pork chops, 1/2-inch thick
1/2 cup vegetable oil
1 teaspoon garlic salt
1 teaspoon paprika

1 teaspoon granulated sugar
1 teaspoon salt
Juice of 2 lemons
   (about 6 tablespoons)

Lay pork chops flat in 2- to 4-quart resealable plastic bag. In a medium bowl, combine oil, garlic salt, paprika, sugar, salt and lemon juice; pour over chops. Seal bag and turn several times to coat meat. Lay bag flat in freezer. Freeze.

When ready to use, thaw pork chops in plastic bag. Remove meat from marinade, reserving marinade. Put marinade in a medium saucepan and heat to boiling. Reduce heat and let marinade simmer until needed.

Place pork chops on gas grill over medium heat or on charcoal grill 4 to 6 inches from medium coals. Cook 5 to 10 minutes per side, or to desired doneness, turning chops at least once and basting occasionally with heated marinade. Discard remaining marinade.

Flank Steak Appetizer

Janet Geissler
Food Editor, *Lansing State Journal*, Lansing, MI

When you think of grilled meats, a juicy steak dinner might be the first thing that pops into mind. But why limit grilling to entrées — or even a side dish of grilled veggies? Why not start your outdoor feast with a grilled hors d'oeuvre? This marinade turns flank steak into a delicious appetizer.

Makes 12 to 16 servings

1 cup water
3/4 cup soy sauce
2 tablespoons Worcestershire sauce
1 teaspoon salt
1 teaspoon granulated sugar

2 cloves garlic, minced
1/8 teaspoon ground ginger
1 beef flank steak
(about 1 1/2 pounds)

In a medium bowl, combine water, soy sauce, Worcestershire sauce, salt, sugar, garlic and ginger; mix well. Reserve 1 cup soy sauce mixture for sauce.

Put meat in shallow dish; pour remaining soy sauce mixture over meat. Refrigerate, covered, at least 8 hours, or overnight; turn meat occasionally.

Remove meat from marinade; discard marinade. Place meat on gas grill over medium-high heat or on charcoal grill 3 inches from medium-hot coals. Cook 4 minutes per side for rare, 8 minutes per side for well done, or until done as desired.

Cut grilled meat into thin diagonal slices. Place meat in a chafing dish with reserved 1 cup soy sauce mixture; stir until heated through. Serve warm as an appetizer.

Note: If you prefer, cut thicker slices of meat to serve as an entrée. Heat reserved 1 cup soy sauce mixture and serve it alongside the steak.

"Impaired" means a person's ability to drive safely is diminished by alcohol or other drugs.

Foiled Franks

Christine Randall
Assistant Features Editor, *The Post and Courier*, Charleston, SC

If you're planning a child's birthday party, consider having a backyard cookout. The kids can run and yell to their hearts' content in the yard. Meanwhile, you can take it easy and just plop these prepared hot dogs on the grill.

Makes 8 servings

3 tablespoons butter or margarine
8 hot dog buns, split
8 hot dogs
1/2 cup pickle relish
1/2 cup ketchup

1/2 cup chopped onion
2 tablespoons prepared
　yellow mustard
Dash hot pepper sauce (optional)

Lightly spread butter on buns. Place each bun on a square of aluminum foil, buttered-side open and up.

Cut hot dogs into 1/4-inch slices. In a medium mixing bowl, combine hot dog slices, pickle relish, ketchup, onion, mustard and hot pepper sauce; mix well. Place an equal amount of hot dog mixture on each bun; close bun. Wrap filled buns in foil.

Place foil packets on gas grill over medium heat or on charcoal grill 4 to 6 inches from medium coals. Cook 10 to 15 minutes, or until heated through. Remove foil before serving to children.

Garlic Steak Sandwiches

Jeanne Voltz
Cookbook Author, Pittsboro, NC

These sandwiches look like whoppers, but we carve the meat thin, so a modest serving seems heartier than it is. The garlic-buttered toasted buns and thick onion slices lend heft at small caloric expense.

Makes 8 servings

1/4 cup margarine or
    butter, softened
4 cloves garlic, minced
2 pounds beef top round steak
    (London broil), in one piece
16 thick slices onion
    (centers of 2 or 3 onions)

8 sandwich buns
    (round or oblong), split
Sliced tomatoes and
    arugula (optional)

In a small bowl, beat margarine until fluffy; blend in garlic to make garlic "butter." Set aside until ready to use or refrigerate up to 3 or 4 days and bring to spreadable temperature before using.

Let steak warm at room temperature 30 minutes before grilling. Trim off excess fat. Spread 1 teaspoon garlic butter on each side of steak.

Place steak on gas grill over high heat or on charcoal grill 4 to 6 inches from hot coals. Cook 10 minutes, or until browned. Turn steak. Lightly spread garlic butter on top and place onion slices on steak. Cook until steak is browned and done as desired, basting once with garlic butter. Cooking will take about 15 minutes for medium-rare.

Place steak on a carving board. Open buns; spread remaining garlic butter on buns. Grill buns until lightly browned.

If onions are not browned to your taste, place them on grill, using tongs or a spatula, and let them brown while you carve the meat.

Cut the steak across the grain into thin slices. Arrange slices on bottom halves of buns; top meat with onions, and, if desired, tomato slices and arugula. Close sandwiches with tops of buns; cut each sandwich in half and serve.

Even one drink can affect a person's ability to drive safely.

Great Balls of Fire

Beth Whitley Duke
Food Editor, *Amarillo Globe-News*, Amarillo, TX

In Texas, if someone warns you that something is hot, you ask them to be more specific: Hot with heat (temperature) or hot with fire (seasonings)? The heat in this recipe comes from hot peppers inside the meatballs. Some brands of canned peppers now come with a "temperature gauge" printed on the label, so you can select the peppers according to the amount of heat you want. If you use fresh peppers, though, you won't know how hot the final product is until you bite into it. As a buyer for Pace picante sauce in San Antonio once told me: "Peppers are like spouses. You never know what kind you have until it's too late."

Makes 6 to 8 servings

12 jalapeño peppers, fresh or
   canned (not pickled)
2 pounds lean ground beef
   (round or chuck)

Taco sauce (optional)

Cut jalapeño peppers into generous chunks, about 1-inch thick. Remove seeds, if desired. Using your hands, form a 1½-inch ball of ground beef around each jalapeño chunk. Using metal skewers, skewer the meatballs so the skewer pierces the pepper and holds the meat in place.

Place skewers on gas grill over high heat or on charcoal grill 4 to 6 inches from hot coals. Cook 18 to 20 minutes, or until well done, turning skewers every 5 minutes. For even hotter meatballs, baste with taco sauce during last 5 minutes of cooking.

Grilled Ham

Sally Scherer
Food Writer, *The Macon Telegraph*, Macon, GA

Ham on the grill? I had never tried it until a friend introduced me to this tasty recipe. The flavorful marinade is both sweet and slightly sour. It reminds me of one my mother used on her Easter hams. I serve this with steamed carrots, salad and bread. It's yummy.

Makes 4 servings

2 slices cooked ham, 1-inch thick
   (about 1 1/2 pounds)
1 cup ginger ale
1 cup orange juice
1/2 cup firmly packed brown sugar

1/4 cup vegetable oil
4 teaspoons cider vinegar
2 teaspoons dry mustard
1/2 teaspoon ground ginger
1/4 teaspoon ground cloves

Score (or remove) fat around edge of ham slices. Place ham in a shallow dish.

In a medium mixing bowl, combine ginger ale, orange juice, brown sugar, oil, vinegar, dry mustard, ginger and cloves; mix well. Pour over ham. Refrigerate, covered, 1 hour, spooning marinade over ham several times.

Remove ham from marinade; reserve marinade. Put marinade in a medium saucepan and heat to boiling. Reduce heat and let marinade simmer until needed.

Place ham on gas grill over low heat or on charcoal grill 4 to 6 inches from low coals. Cook about 15 minutes on each side, brushing with heated marinade frequently. Serve remaining heated marinade as a sauce with ham.

Cold showers, coffee, or fresh air won't sober up a drunk — only time will help.

Grilled Lamb Kebabs

Carolyn Flournoy
Food Columnist, *The Times*, Shreveport, LA

Grilling kebabs makes an outdoor meal seem festive. Better yet, you can marinate the kebabs in advance, so at mealtime all you have to do is put the meat on the skewers. I introduced my children to lamb with this recipe. Now they request lamb kebabs for their birthday dinners.

Makes 6 servings

1 cup chopped onions
3 cloves garlic, minced
2/3 cup cider vinegar
1/4 cup vegetable oil
1/4 cup olive oil
3 tablespoons honey
1 tablespoon dried rosemary
2 teaspoons chopped fresh mint

1/2 teaspoon salt
1/2 teaspoon seasoned pepper
2 pounds boneless lamb, cut
   into 24 cubes
1 large onion, cut into 12
   wedges and halved
12 plum tomatoes, halved
24 small fresh mushrooms

In a shallow dish, combine chopped onions, garlic, vinegar, vegetable oil, olive oil, honey, rosemary, mint, salt and pepper; mix well. Add lamb cubes; stir to coat evenly. Refrigerate, covered, 6 to 8 hours; stir occasionally.

When ready to grill, drain meat, reserving marinade. Put marinade in a medium saucepan and heat to boiling. Reduce heat and let marinade simmer until needed.

On each of 6 metal skewers, thread 1 piece onion, 1 meat cube, 1 tomato half and 1 mushroom; repeat 3 times.

Place kebabs on a gas grill over medium-high heat or on charcoal grill 4 to 6 inches from medium-hot coals. Cook 12 to 15 minutes, basting several times with heated marinade. Discard remaining marinade.

Grilled Leg of Lamb

Narcisse S. Cadgène
Free-Lance Writer, New York, NY

Nothing, but nothing, beats a barbecued butterflied leg of lamb. When important company — meaning clients or in-laws — come to visit, I know I can count on this to wow 'em.

Makes 6 to 8 servings

1 boneless leg of lamb, trimmed
   (about 4 to 5 pounds bone-in,
   3 pounds boned)
1 jar (12 ounces) chutney
1 medium-size red apple, unpeeled,
   cored and cubed

2 tablespoons honey
2 tablespoons cider vinegar
2 cloves garlic, cut into quarters
1/2 teaspoon black pepper, or to taste

Lay the leg of lamb out flat and pound the thickest areas with a mallet or heavy skillet until the meat is 2 to 3 inches thick. This will promote even cooking of the lamb.

Place the chutney, apple, honey, vinegar, garlic and pepper in the bowl of a food processor fitted with a steel blade (or in container of electric blender); process until the mixture is well combined, but still chunky. Taste; add more pepper, if desired. Remove about 1/2 cup of the mixture; reserve to serve as a condiment with the meat. Process remaining mixture until it is a fairly uniform purée.

Coat the lamb with about half the puréed chutney mixture. Let marinate 1 hour at room temperature, or longer in the refrigerator (preferably overnight). Remove lamb from marinade; discard marinade. Place lamb on gas grill over high heat or on charcoal grill 4 to 6 inches from hot coals. Cook 4 to 5 minutes per side to sear. Reduce heat to medium-low or move lamb away from hottest coals. Cook 15 to 20 minutes, basting liberally with remaining puréed chutney mixture and turning every 5 minutes. Check the internal temperature after 10 minutes. Lamb is medium rare when the internal temperature reaches 140° and medium at 150°. Discard remaining purée.

Let the lamb rest 5 minutes before slicing. Cut thin slices against the grain, as for London broil. Serve with reserved 1/2 cup chunky sauce.

It's a fact: alcohol is a drug.

Ham Burgers

Toni Burks
Free-Lance Writer, Roanoke, VA

Forget the predictable casserole when you have ham leftovers. Grind the lean meat in a food processor, add some ingredients that bind, shape the mixture into patties and cook them on the grill.

Makes 6 servings

1/2 cup orange marmalade
1/8 teaspoon ground ginger
1/4 teaspoon dry mustard
1 slice white bread
1 egg, beaten
1 tablespoon orange juice, water or milk

2 tablespoons chopped onion
1 tablespoon chopped fresh parsley
Dash ground ginger
3 cups coarsely chopped or ground cooked smoked ham
Hamburger buns, split (optional)

In small saucepan, combine orange marmalade, 1/8 teaspoon ginger and dry mustard. Cook over low heat until marmalade is melted and bubbly. Remove from heat; set aside.

Remove crust from bread; discard crust. Crumble bread into fine crumbs. In a medium mixing bowl, combine bread crumbs, egg, orange juice, onion, parsley and a dash of ginger. Add ham; mix well. Divide mixture into 6 equal portions; shape into patties.

Place patties on gas grill over medium-high heat or on charcoal grill 4 to 6 inches from medium-hot coals. Cook 5 minutes. Turn and brush with marmalade sauce. Cook 5 to 6 minutes, or until heated through. Brush with marmalade sauce just before serving. Serve on hamburger buns, if desired. Discard remaining marmalade sauce.

Hot Dogs — Your Way

Carolyn Flournoy
Food Columnist, *The Times*, Shreveport, LA

> *One of my favorite ways to feed neighbors, the Scout troop, the Sunday school class or drop-in friends is Hot Dogs — Your Way. I devised this method years ago when it seemed each of our four children wanted hot dogs cooked a different way. I prepare the toppings early in the day (or the night before), then sit back and let everyone grill the franks and select the toppings of choice.*

Makes 16 to 20 servings

Muffuletta Topping
(see recipe)
Chili Topping
(see recipe)
Rueben Topping
(see recipe)

2 pounds hot dogs
   (8 or 10 per one-pound
   package)
16 to 20 hot dog buns
Prepared yellow mustard

Prepare toppings.

When ready to grill, place hot dogs on gas grill over medium heat or on charcoal grill 4 to 6 inches from medium coals. Cook 8 to 10 minutes, turning once with tongs. Serve in buns with desired topping(s). Have plain mustard available for the purists.

Muffuletta Topping

3/4 cup chopped celery
1/2 cup sliced pimento-stuffed
   olives
1/4 cup finely chopped carrot
1 clove garlic, minced

1 tablespoon capers
1/4 cup olive oil
2 teaspoons balsamic vinegar
1/2 teaspoon Italian herb
   seasoning

In a medium bowl, combine celery, olives, carrot, garlic, capers, olive oil, vinegar and Italian herb seasoning; mix well. Refrigerate, covered, until ready to serve.

Place grilled hot dog in bun; top with about 1/4 cup topping. Makes enough for 8 to 10 hot dogs.

It is time to treat drunk driving as a serious crime.

Chili Topping

1 can (16 ounces) chili
  without beans
Prepared yellow mustard

1/2 cup sliced green onions
1 cup grated Cheddar cheese

Put chili in a saucepan; set it on the grill along with the hot dogs. Heat until almost boiling, stirring occasionally. Spread mustard on bun; place grilled hot dog in bun. Spoon about 1/4 cup chili over hot dog; sprinkle green onions and cheese on chili. Makes enough for 8 to 10 hot dogs.

Reuben Topping

3/4 cup bottled Thousand Island
  salad dressing
4 slices Swiss cheese, cut
  in quarters

1 small green bell pepper, cut in
  rings and halved
1 cup sauerkraut, rinsed and
  drained

Spread salad dressing on hot dog buns. Place grilled hot dog, cheese and green pepper in bun; top with sauerkraut. Makes enough for 8 to 10 hot dogs.

Kiwi Venison Steaks

Clara H. Eschmann
Food Columnist, *The Macon Telegraph*, Macon, GA

My son grows peanuts on a farm in southwest Georgia. He hunts deer on the farm during hunting season. Consequently, he has experimented with a number of venison recipes, including ones for grilling. I was glad to pass on a tip to him about tenderizing meat with ripe kiwifruit. Kiwis not only make the meat less tough, but they also add a light sweet flavor.

Makes 8 servings

8 venison steaks
3 to 4 very ripe kiwifruit
Salt and black pepper, to taste
About 3 tablespoons
   Worcestershire sauce

16 slices bacon, halved
1/2 cup finely chopped onion

Pound steaks with meat mallet to make cube steaks. Peel and mash kiwis. Generously rub mashed kiwifruit on both sides of each steak; steaks should be well coated. (The number of kiwis needed will depend on size.) Season each steak with salt and pepper. Sprinkle about 1 teaspoon Worcestershire sauce on each steak. Place two pieces of bacon on one side of each steak; secure bacon with wooden picks.

Place steaks, bacon-side up, on gas grill over medium heat or on charcoal grill 4 inches from medium coals. Cook 5 to 6 minutes. Turn steaks. Sprinkle onion on cooked side of meat. Top each steak with 2 pieces of remaining bacon. Cook 6 to 10 minutes, or until meat is fork-tender, bacon is cooked and onions are soft. (Coals will become cooler during cooking time, but drippings from bacon might increase the heat. It might be necessary to reduce the heat or scatter the coals.) Serve immediately.

Ask what police, judges and lawmakers are doing to end drunk driving.

Lamb Steaks Supreme

Sally Scherer
Food Writer, *The Macon Telegraph*, Macon, GA

Lamb isn't the most popular meat for grilling, but with this recipe you might want to consider grilling lamb more often. The longer the meat marinates, the better the flavor. However, even if it marinates only a short time, the meat seems to pick up the delicious flavor. A crisp, green salad and warm bread are good accompaniments to these steaks.

Makes 4 servings

2 lamb leg steaks, 3/4-inch thick
   (about 1 pound)
1/2 cup cold, strong coffee
1/4 cup brown sugar
2 tablespoons lemon juice

1 tablespoon prepared
   yellow mustard
1/2 teaspoon Worcestershire
   sauce
1 clove garlic, minced

Place steaks in a single layer in a shallow dish. In a small mixing bowl, combine coffee, brown sugar, lemon juice, mustard, Worcestershire sauce and garlic; mix well. Pour sauce over lamb. Refrigerate, covered, at least 1 hour, turning steaks several times.

Remove steaks from marinade; reserve marinade. Put marinade in a medium saucepan and heat to boiling. Reduce heat and let marinade simmer until needed.

Place steaks on gas grill over high heat or on charcoal grill 4 inches over hot coals. Cook, basting often with heated marinade, about 6 minutes per side, or to desired doneness. Discard remaining marinade.

Lemon-Herb Rabbit

Jeanne Voltz
Cookbook Author, Pittsboro, NC

The delicate flavor of domestic rabbit is brought out by basting with a not-too-spicy sauce. You may be able to find someone who sells fresh rabbits, especially in the country. The woman we buy from raises her stock in hutches in her backyard, and dresses the meat beautifully. The frozen rabbit in supermarkets is good, too; just thaw in the refrigerator before cooking.

Makes 4 servings

1 rabbit (2¹/₂ pounds), dressed
    and cut into quarters
    (thaw, if frozen)
1 lemon, halved
Salt and black pepper, to taste
1 tablespoon minced fresh tarragon,
    rosemary, thyme, basil or dill
    (or 1 teaspoon dried)

1 teaspoon Dijon-style mustard
¹/₂ teaspoon granulated sugar
3 tablespoons olive oil
    or vegetable oil
2 tablespoons fresh lemon juice

Rub rabbit pieces with cut lemon; lightly season with salt and pepper. Let stand 15 to 20 minutes.

In a small bowl, combine herb of choice, mustard and sugar; mix well. Whisk in oil. Add lemon juice and mix well.

Place rabbit, meaty-side down, on gas grill over high heat or on charcoal grill 5 to 6 inches from hot coals. Lightly brush with herb sauce. Cook 5 minutes, or until browned. Turn; baste again with herb sauce. Cook about 45 minutes, turning and basting to cook evenly. With a small sharp knife, cut deeply into a joint. If the juice is pink, grill 10 to 15 minutes longer, or until juice runs clear. Discard remaining herb sauce.

Place rabbit on a platter. Serve with barbecue sauce, fruit sauce or relish of your choice.

Vote for tougher drunk driving laws.

Manhattan Steak

Jim Hillibish
City Editor, *The Repository*, Canton, OH

Thickly cut steak, beautifully tender, benefits from a glaze-type barbecue sauce that seals in the meat's juices. The sugar in the ketchup of this sauce chars slightly, creating an appetizing appearance, complete with grilling marks. The roots of this sauce are in the mid-town Manhattan grill rooms of the 1930s, where steaks were cooked to order in front of patrons.

Makes 4 servings

1/4 cup butter or margarine	1 teaspoon lemon-pepper seasoning
1 medium onion, finely chopped	1 teaspoon dry mustard
1 clove garlic, minced	1/2 teaspoon cayenne pepper
1 cup ketchup	5 to 6 drops hot pepper sauce
1/4 cup beef broth	4 thick-cut Porterhouse or
1 tablespoon Worcestershire sauce	T-bone beef steaks
1 tablespoon white vinegar	

Melt butter in a small saucepan. Add onion and garlic; cook 1 minute. Add ketchup, broth, Worcestershire sauce, vinegar, lemon pepper, dry mustard, cayenne and hot pepper sauce; mix well. Bring mixture to a boil. Reduce heat; simmer 10 minutes, stirring often.

Place steaks on gas grill over medium heat or on charcoal grill 4 inches from medium coals. Brush with sauce. Cook 15 to 20 minutes for rare to medium, or until done as desired, turning and basting with sauce. Discard remaining sauce.

Note: Do not salt steaks. The sauce is flavoring enough.

Midwest-Style Spareribs

Ann Corell Wells
Food Editor, *The Grand Rapids Press*, Grand Rapids, MI

Grilling is a year-round cooking experience for me — in the sun, snow or rain. However, as often as I grill, I have few recipes. I create most marinades and basting sauces as I go, but this is one recipe I do use. The original recipe, which I found years ago in a cookbook and have changed, called for spareribs, but the sauce is just as tasty on pork chops, pork loin roast, pork tenderloin or chicken. Many recipes call for parboiling or baking ribs before grilling, however I prefer to put the uncooked ribs on the grill over medium heat and cook them longer. Because some members of my family prefer ribs seasoned with just salt and pepper, I often make the sauce and serve it on the side for dipping the ribs. Delicious!

Makes 6 servings

6 cloves garlic, minced
1 1/2 teaspoons seasoned salt
1/2 teaspoon coarsely ground
   black pepper
3 racks pork spareribs
   (about 6 to 7 pounds)

1 cup firmly packed brown sugar
3/4 to 1 cup coarse-grain mustard
1/4 cup molasses or honey
1/2 teaspoon dry mustard

In a small bowl, combine garlic, salt and pepper; rub on spareribs. Place ribs on gas grill over medium heat or on charcoal grill 4 to 6 inches from medium coals. Cook, covered, 45 to 60 minutes, or to desired doneness; turn ribs often.

In a saucepan, combine brown sugar, coarse-grain mustard, molasses and dry mustard. Bring to a boil. Reduce heat; simmer about 5 minutes, or until sugar is dissolved. Sauce can be made in advance and refrigerated or left at room temperature.

About 15 minutes before the ribs are done, brush some of the sauce on the bony side of the ribs. Cook 5 minutes, or until crispy; turn ribs and brush meaty side with sauce. Cook 5 minutes, or until crispy. (Or, grill seasoned ribs and serve sauce on the side for dipping.)

MADD is working to lower the BAC limit for adults to .08 in all states.

Okie Dokie Barbecued Bologna

Paula M. Galusha
Free-Lance Home Economist, Tulsa, OK

When young teens get together for an outdoor barbecue, it's fun to serve something besides the usual hamburgers and hot dogs. This barbecue sauce can be used for ham or chicken, as well as the bologna called for in this recipe. Because Oklahomans can barbecue nine months out of the year, I keep this recipe handy.

Makes 10 to 12 servings

4 pounds bologna, unsliced
Whole cloves
1 cup unsulphured molasses
1/2 cup prepared yellow mustard

6 tablespoons red wine vinegar
1 teaspoon grated orange peel
Hamburger buns, split and toasted

Remove any casing from bologna; score meat in diamond pattern. Insert cloves into meat where score lines cross.

Place bologna on gas grill over low heat or on charcoal grill 4 to 6 inches from low coals. Cook 30 minutes, turning frequently.

Meanwhile, in a mixing bowl, combine molasses, mustard, vinegar and orange peel; mix well. After bologna has cooked 30 minutes, baste bologna with molasses mixture. Cook 15 to 20 minutes, or until done as desired, basting frequently.

Slice grilled bologna into thick slices. Serve on toasted hamburger buns; top with remaining molasses mixture.

Plum Delicious Ribs

Janet Geissler
Food Editor, *Lansing State Journal*, Lansing, MI

These barbecued ribs are plum delicious! That's because the sauce is made with plums. Because plums are available canned, you don't have to wait until late summer, when plums come into season, to prepare this recipe. You'll want to try this as soon as your grilling season begins — and for a growing number of people, that's all year long.

Makes 8 to 10 servings

8 to 10 pounds pork spareribs	1/4 cup chili sauce
Salted water	1/4 cup soy sauce
2 tablespoons margarine	2 teaspoons prepared
1/2 cup chopped onions	yellow mustard
1 can (17 ounces) purple plums	1 teaspoon ground ginger
1 can (6 ounces) frozen lemonade	1 teaspoon Worcestershire sauce
concentrate, thawed, undiluted	

Cut ribs into serving portions of 2 or 3 ribs each. Put ribs in a large Dutch oven or stockpot; cover with salted water. Simmer 45 to 50 minutes, or until ribs are tender; drain.

In a large saucepan, melt margarine. Add onions; sauté until tender. Drain plums, reserving syrup; remove and discard pits. Place plums and reserved syrup in container of electric blender or food processor; cover and blend until smooth. Add puréed plums to onions; mix well. Add lemonade concentrate, chili sauce, soy sauce, mustard, ginger and Worcestershire sauce; mix well. Simmer, uncovered, 10 to 15 minutes, stirring occasionally. Let simmer until needed.

Place ribs on gas grill over low heat or on charcoal grill 4 to 6 inches from low coals. Cook 25 minutes, or until done; turn ribs 3 or 4 times and baste frequently with plum sauce. Serve ribs with remaining plum sauce.

Find out how your state "rates" on drunk driving legislation.

Reubenburgers

Debra Carr-Elsing
Food Writer, *The Capital Times*, Madison, WI

Here's a recipe that's modeled after the famous Reuben sandwich. I like recipes that have an element of surprise, and there's plenty of that here. When you bite into the burger, you get a mouthful of creamy Swiss cheese. It's a delightful twist. Plus, kids have fun helping mound the grated cheese on beef patties, then sealing the surprise inside.

Makes 6 servings

1 tablespoon vegetable oil
1 small onion, chopped
1 1/2 cups sauerkraut,
   rinsed and drained
1/2 cup apple juice or beef broth
1/3 cup ketchup
2 pounds lean ground beef

2 tablespoons prepared
   yellow mustard
1/4 teaspoon salt
1 cup shredded Swiss cheese
   (about 4 ounces)
6 hamburger buns, split

Heat oil in a medium skillet. Add onion; sauté until lightly browned. Stir in sauerkraut, apple juice and ketchup. Simmer, uncovered, 20 minutes. Keep warm.

In a medium mixing bowl, combine ground beef, mustard and salt; shape into 12 thin patties. Place an equal amount of cheese on each of 6 patties. Top each with a second patty; seal edges to hold in cheese filling.

Place on gas grill over medium-high heat or on charcoal grill 5 to 6 inches from medium-hot coals. Cook 6 to 8 minutes per side, or until well done. Place hamburger buns, cut-side down, around edges of grill 3 or 4 minutes to toast. Serve burgers on toasted buns, topped with warm sauerkraut mixture.

Seasoned Steak with Grilled Peppers

Mary Beth Jung
Free-Lance Writer, Grafton, WI

If you haven't tasted the dry marinades, also called rubs, here's an easy recipe to try. The secret of this technique is to let the dry herbs "marinate" the meat. The moisture from the meat triggers an explosion of flavor from the herbs. If you're watching your salt intake, simply omit the salt and let the herbs season the meat.

Makes 4 servings

2 teaspoons freshly cracked black pepper
2 teaspoons dried basil
1 teaspoon dried thyme
1 teaspoon dried oregano
1 teaspoon salt (optional)

Dash cayenne pepper
4 T-bone or Porterhouse beef steaks
1 each red, green and yellow bell peppers, seeded and quartered
Olive oil

In a small bowl, combine pepper, basil, thyme, oregano, salt and cayenne. Rub seasoning mixture over both sides of each steak. Refrigerate, covered, several hours.

Place steaks on gas grill over medium-high heat or on charcoal grill 4 to 6 inches from medium-hot coals. Cook steaks, turning occasionally, 15 to 20 minutes for rare to medium, or until done as desired. About 5 minutes before steaks are done, brush bell peppers with olive oil and place peppers on the grill. Cook peppers, turning occasionally, about 5 minutes, or until tender; do not overcook. Serve steaks topped with grilled peppers.

Drunk driving crashes are never accidents.

Sour Cream Beef Burgers

Sally Scherer
Food Writer, *The Macon Telegraph*, Macon, GA

Why settle for plain burgers when you can add a few ingredients, such as green onion, sour cream and bread crumbs, and enjoy extra-special, delicious burgers? These hamburgers are moist and flavorful with a texture that's similar to meat loaf.

Makes 4 servings

1 1/2 pounds lean ground beef
1 cup coarse fresh bread crumbs
4 green onions, finely chopped
1/3 cup sour cream

3 teaspoons Worcestershire sauce
1/2 teaspoon salt
1/2 teaspoon black pepper

In a large mixing bowl, combine ground beef, bread crumbs, green onions, sour cream, Worcestershire sauce, salt and pepper; mix thoroughly. Shape mixture into 4 patties.

Place patties on gas grill over medium-high heat or on charcoal grill 4 to 6 inches from medium-hot coals. Cook 6 to 8 minutes per side, or until well done. Serve on hamburger buns with an assortment of condiments, if desired.

South African Safari Kebabs

Barbara Gibbs Ostmann
Food Writer, St. Louis, MO

On a flying safari of game reserves in South Africa in late 1993, we were awed by the magnificent wildlife. At each of the Conservation Corporation lodges where we stayed, the daily menus featured game and local specialties along with more familiar European-type cuisine. At Londolozi Game Reserve, for example, we sampled mealie pap (maize meal), boerewors (local pork sausages) and biltong (ostrich jerky). Venison sosaties turned out to be kebabs of impala or other game similar to our deer or antelope. You can use this basic marinade for venison — either wild or farm-raised — or for impala, if you happen to have it.

Makes 4 servings

1 pound boneless venison
    loin or roast
1/4 cup red wine vinegar
2 tablespoons vegetable oil
1/4 cup ketchup
2 teaspoons Worcestershire sauce

1 teaspoon granulated sugar
1 clove garlic, finely chopped
1/2 teaspoon dry mustard
1/4 teaspoon salt
1/4 teaspoon black pepper

Trim all fat and connective tissue from venison. Cut into long thin strips, to thread on skewers. (If preferred, cut into 1-inch cubes.) Put meat in a resealable plastic bag and put bag in a large bowl.

In a small bowl, combine vinegar, oil, ketchup, Worcestershire sauce, sugar, garlic, dry mustard, salt and pepper; mix well. Pour over meat in bag. Close bag and turn several times to coat meat. Refrigerate 4 to 6 hours, or overnight, turning occasionally.

Remove meat from marinade; reserve marinade. Put reserved marinade in a saucepan and heat to boiling. Reduce heat and let marinade simmer until needed.

Thread meat strips (or cubes) on metal skewers. Place on gas grill over medium heat or on charcoal grill 4 to 6 inches from medium coals. Cook 5 to 8 minutes; brush with heated marinade and turn. Cook other side 5 to 8 minutes, or until done as desired. Baste again with heated marinade. Serve hot. Discard remaining marinade.

Alcohol and other drug-impaired driving is no joke.

Spiedini Sandwiches

Mary Beth Jung
Free-Lance Writer, Grafton, WI

When a hearty sandwich is in order, try this easy recipe. Use your choice of beef, pork, lamb, chicken, turkey or even venison. I like to serve the grilled meat on crusty French rolls. To assemble a sandwich, simply slice a roll, place a skewer of grilled meat inside the roll, hold the roll around the meat and pull the meat from the skewer.

Makes 6 to 8 servings

1 cup vegetable oil
2/3 cup cider vinegar
2 tablespoons Worcestershire sauce
1/2 medium onion, chopped
1/2 teaspoon salt
1/2 teaspoon granulated sugar
1/2 teaspoon dried basil
1/2 teaspoon dried marjoram
1/2 teaspoon dried rosemary
2 1/2 pounds boneless pork, beef or other meat, cut into 1-inch cubes
Italian rolls or small French bread baguettes

In a shallow dish, combine oil, vinegar, Worcestershire sauce, onion, salt, sugar, basil, marjoram and rosemary; mix well. Add meat cubes to oil mixture; toss to coat meat. Refrigerate, covered, overnight, stirring mixture several times.

When ready to grill, thread meat cubes on metal skewers; discard marinade.

Place skewers on gas grill over high heat or on charcoal grill 4 to 6 inches from hot coals. Cook 10 to 15 minutes, or until done as desired. Remove meat from skewers; serve on rolls.

St. Louis Pork Steaks

Barbara Gibbs Ostmann
Food Writer, St. Louis, MO

Warm weather and outdoor cooking go together like St. Louis and Cardinals baseball. And in St. Louis, outdoor cooking is synonymous with pork steaks, a local favorite. I'd never even heard of them until I moved here in the '70s to become food editor at the St. Louis Post-Dispatch. *Back home in Arkansas, we ate pork chops, but not pork steaks. My husband grew up on pork steaks, however, and he usually does the honors at the grill.*

Makes 4 servings

4 pork steaks,
　　1- to 1¼-inches thick
½ cup bottled barbecue sauce
　　(your favorite)
⅓ cup honey

1 tablespoon Worcestershire sauce
1 teaspoon garlic salt
½ teaspoon prepared
　　yellow mustard

Pound pork steaks with a meat mallet. For basting sauce, combine barbecue sauce, honey, Worcestershire sauce, garlic salt and mustard in a small bowl; mix well.

Place steaks on gas grill over medium heat or on charcoal grill about 4 inches from medium-low coals. Cook about 8 minutes on each side. Baste liberally with sauce. Cook 5 minutes more, or until done as desired, turning and basting frequently with sauce. Discard remaining sauce.

Tell the young people in your life that the national drinking age is 21.

Texas-Style Ribs

Beth Whitley Duke
Food Editor, *Amarillo Globe-News*, Amarillo, TX

If you look under "B" in the Yellow Pages in most Texas telephone books, you'll find long listings under Baptist Churches and Barbecue. In fact, many Texas cooks take their barbecue so seriously, it might as well be a religion. Famous barbecue restaurants copyright their barbecue sauce recipes and guard the secret ingredients more closely than they guard their cash registers. Most Texans prefer traditional beef or pork ribs. Baby back ribs are still relative newcomers to Texas. This recipe calls for country-style ribs, which are meatier than spareribs and excellent for grilling.

Makes 6 to 8 servings

1 medium onion, chopped
1 cup soy sauce
1 cup firmly packed brown sugar
1/2 cup cider vinegar
1/4 cup ketchup
2 tablespoons prepared
   yellow mustard

10 pounds country-style pork ribs
   (average serving is two ribs
   per person)
Bottled barbecue sauce, for
   basting (optional)

In a medium bowl, combine onion, soy sauce, brown sugar, vinegar, ketchup and mustard; mix well.

Spray a 13x9x2-inch baking dish with nonstick cooking spray. Place ribs side by side with bone on top. Do not crowd the ribs. Use a second baking dish, if needed, to allow space between ribs for the marinade. Gently pour the marinade over ribs, making sure it gets in the spaces between the ribs. Refrigerate, covered, 4 to 6 hours, or preferably overnight.

Remove cover from baking dish. Do not drain ribs. Bake ribs in a preheated 350° oven 30 minutes.

Remove ribs from oven; drain marinade and accumulated fat and discard. Place ribs on gas grill over medium heat or on charcoal grill 4 inches from medium coals. Cook 20 to 25 minutes, turning halfway through cooking. If desired, baste ribs with your favorite barbecue sauce during the last 5 minutes of cooking.

The Perfect Burger

Eleanor Ostman
Food Writer, *St. Paul Pioneer Press*, St. Paul, MN

In California, they put the vegetables on their hamburgers. In France, where this recipe originated, they put them in the burgers, and the results are fabulous. Even the mustard and tomato flavors are built-in. These burgers can be grilled or cooked in a cast-iron skillet. We serve them with choices of lettuce, tomatoes and cheese, but the burgers are grand without any additional garnishment. We think a hamburger like this deserves a grilled buttered bun.

Makes 12 to 16 servings

2 eggs
1/2 cup finely chopped celery
1/2 cup finely chopped onions
1 tomato, peeled and finely chopped
1 teaspoon chili powder
1 tablespoon Worcestershire sauce
1 teaspoon Dijon-style mustard,
   or more, to taste

Salt and black pepper, to taste
4 pounds extra-lean ground beef
Hamburger buns
Butter (optional)
Lettuce, sliced tomatoes and sliced
   cheese (optional toppings)

In a large mixing bowl, combine eggs, celery, onions, tomato, chili powder, Worcestershire sauce, mustard, salt and pepper; mix well. Add beef; blend well. Shape mixture into 12 to 16 patties.

Place patties on gas grill over medium heat or on charcoal grill 4 to 6 inches from medium coals. Cook, turning once, 14 to 18 minutes, or until well done.

Split buns, lightly butter (if desired), and toast on grill. Serve burgers plain on toasted buns, or add toppings of choice.

The minimum drinking age of 21 saved about 819 lives in 1993.

Tulsa Kebabs

Paula M. Galusha
Free-Lance Home Economist, Tulsa, OK

When the summer temperature reaches 100°, you don't want to be outside in the heat by a hot grill for long. Kebabs are a favorite in Tulsa because they cook quickly. My family likes these kebabs because they taste great, and I like them because I can have a meal on the table in less than an hour.

Makes 4 to 6 servings

1 cup soy sauce
1/2 cup water
3 tablespoons Worcestershire sauce
3 tablespoons brown sugar
1 tablespoon grated onion
1 clove garlic, minced
1/2 teaspoon dry mustard
2 pounds beef sirloin, cut into
   1-inch cubes

1 pound medium-size
   fresh mushrooms
4 small zucchini, cut into 1-inch slices
2 pints cherry tomatoes,
   rinsed and drained
Hot cooked rice

In a shallow dish or plastic bag, combine soy sauce, water, Worcestershire sauce, brown sugar, onion, garlic and dry mustard; mix well. Add beef cubes. Let marinate, covered, at room temperature 30 minutes. (Or, refrigerate, covered, several hours, or overnight.)

Remove meat from marinade; reserve marinade. Put reserved marinade in a saucepan and heat to boiling. Reduce heat and let marinade simmer until needed.

Remove stems from mushrooms; discard stems or save for another use. Rinse and drain mushroom caps.

Alternate beef cubes, mushroom caps, zucchini slices and cherry tomatoes on metal skewers. Place kebabs on gas grill over medium heat or on charcoal grill 5 inches from medium-high coals. Brush generously with heated marinade. Cook 7 minutes per side, or until done as desired. Discard remaining marinade. Serve kebabs with rice.

Zesty Flank Steak

Dorothy Cunningham
Free-Lance Writer, Morenci, MI

My husband and I have cut down on the amount of red meat we eat, as have many people. Therefore, when we do treat ourselves to a steak, we want it to be something special. A friend passed along this recipe for grilled flank steak, and it really is special. The mustardy tang and flavorful herbs ensure that each bite is a treat to be remembered.

Makes 8 servings

1 cup mixed mustards
  (see directions)
1/4 cup olive oil
2 teaspoons dried oregano
2 teaspoons dried thyme

2 teaspoons dried basil
1 1/2 teaspoons dried rosemary
4 cloves garlic, minced
1 1/2 to 2 pounds beef flank steak

In a medium mixing bowl, combine any mustards you have on hand, such as Dijon, prepared yellow, horseradish, etc., to make 1 cup. Add olive oil, oregano, thyme, basil, rosemary and garlic to mustard mixture; mix well.

Trim fat from steak. With a brush or spatula, spread a thick coat of mustard mixture on both sides of steak. Discard any remaining mustard mixture. Refrigerate steak, covered, overnight, or at least 3 hours. Remove from refrigerator about 1 hour before grilling.

Place steak on gas grill over high heat or on charcoal grill 4 to 6 inches from hot coals. Cook 5 to 7 minutes on each side, or until done as desired. Place steak on a cutting board; let rest 2 to 3 minutes. Cut in thin diagonal slices. Serve immediately.

Remind all passengers in your car to buckle up.

POULTRY

48   Barbecued Chicken Wings

49   Barbecued Pizza

50   Chicken Kebabs Bombay

51   Chicken Nugget Sandwiches

52   Chicken on the Grill

53   Chicken Tenders in Tangy Mustard Sauce

54   Chili Relleno Chicken

55   Cilantro Grilled Chicken Breast

56   Grilled Quail on Toast

57   Greek-Style Kebabs

58   Herbed Chicken Breasts

59   Honey-Mustard Chicken

60   Kebabs with Jalapeño-Honey Sauce

61   Lemon-Herb Chicken Breasts

62   Lemony Herb Chicken

63   Mexican Chicken

64   Mushroom-Stuffed Chicken Thighs

65   Mustard Barbecued Chicken

66   Spicy Lemon Chicken

67   Turkey Burgers

68   Virgin Islands Grilled Turkey

Barbecued Chicken Wings

Carolyn Flournoy
Food Columnist, *The Times*, Shreveport, LA

A few years ago when Buffalo chicken wings became so popular, I realized we had been barbecuing chicken wings for a long time and, if modesty permits, ours were much better. Our recipe was born of economy and our children's fondness for anything cooked outdoors. A big plus was the fact that the wings could be grilled while I was preparing the rest of dinner — and there were never any leftovers!

Makes 4 to 6 servings

2 tablespoons vegetable oil
1/2 cup finely chopped onion
2 cloves garlic, minced
(or 1/4 teaspoon garlic powder)
1/2 cup ketchup
3 tablespoons cider vinegar

3 tablespoons brown sugar
2 tablespoons lemon juice
2 tablespoons Dijon-style mustard
1 teaspoon hot pepper sauce
1/2 teaspoon salt
12 to 15 chicken wings

In a heavy 3-quart saucepan, heat oil. Add onion; sauté, stirring constantly, about 2 minutes, or until transparent. Add garlic; sauté, stirring, about 20 seconds; do not brown. Add ketchup, vinegar, brown sugar, lemon juice, mustard, hot pepper sauce and salt. Bring to a boil, stirring. Remove from heat.

Put chicken wings in a shallow dish; pour marinade over chicken. Stir to coat chicken evenly. Let chicken marinate while you prepare the grill.

Remove chicken from marinade; discard marinade. Place chicken on gas grill over medium-high heat or charcoal grill 4 to 6 inches from medium-hot coals. Cook 15 to 20 minutes, turning once, or until skin is browned and chicken is done.

Note: This marinade is also good with chicken thighs or chicken quarters.

Tell youngsters how they can "party" safely without alcohol.

Barbecued Pizza

Nancy Ross Ryan
Food Editor, *Restaurants & Institutions*, Des Plaines, IL

Summer or winter, pizza knows no season. But summertime and the outdoor grill provide a chance to enjoy America's favorite pie barbecued. Using a covered grill to cook pizza results in a crispy crust, similar to commercially prepared pizza. Be sure to use regular, not smoky, barbecue sauce, because grilling imparts its own smoky flavor. This pizza is a wonderful way to use up yesterday's leftover barbecued chicken.

Makes 8 servings

Dough for a 14-inch pizza crust
    (use homemade, refrigerated
    or frozen and thawed dough)
1/4 cup barbecue sauce
    (not smoky flavor)
2 1/2 cups shredded Mozzarella
    cheese (about 10 ounces)

1 1/2 cups skinned, shredded
    cooked chicken
1 teaspoon dried oregano
Salt and black pepper, to taste

Use a covered grill that is large enough to hold a 14-inch pizza pan. When coals are red hot, distribute them around periphery of grill. Place grill rack in top position.

While coals are heating, spray a 14-inch metal pizza pan with nonstick cooking spray. Stretch pizza dough to fit pan. Use a rubber spatula to spread barbecue sauce evenly on dough. Sprinkle cheese over sauce. Evenly distribute shredded chicken over cheese. Sprinkle oregano over all. Season with salt and pepper.

Place pizza on rack of prepared grill. Cover grill with lid, leaving top and bottom vents open. Cook 20 minutes, or until pizza crust is golden brown around the edges and cheese is bubbling in the center. Remove from grill. Slide pizza from pan onto a cutting board. Cut into 8 wedges.

Note: One-half pound lean ground beef, cooked, or 1 1/2 cups skinned, chopped, cooked turkey can be substituted for chicken.

Chicken Kebabs Bombay

Laura Barton
Free-Lance Writer, Portland, OR

Yogurt acts as a tangy moistener in marinades. In this recipe, yogurt is combined with flavorful spices that are found in Middle Eastern and Indian cuisines. I like to serve these kebabs with aromatic rice, such as basmati, and a crisp green salad.

Makes 4 servings

2 1/3 pounds chicken, skinned, boned and cut into 1-inch cubes
2 tablespoons ground coriander
2 teaspoons fresh lemon juice
1 1/2 teaspoons freshly grated ginger (or 2 teaspoons ground ginger)
1 teaspoon ground cinnamon
1 teaspoon minced fresh garlic
3/4 teaspoon black pepper
1/2 teaspoon ground cardamom
1/2 cup plain yogurt
1/2 teaspoon chili powder
1/2 teaspoon salt, or to taste
Melted butter

Put chicken cubes in a large shallow dish. Add coriander, lemon juice, ginger, cinnamon, garlic, pepper and cardamom; stir to coat chicken. Refrigerate, covered, 1 hour.

In a small bowl, combine yogurt, chili powder and salt; blend well. Pour over chicken mixture and mix well. Let marinate while you prepare the grill.

Skewer chicken on metal skewers (or wooden skewers that have been soaked in water for 30 minutes). Discard marinade.

Place kebabs on gas grill over medium heat or charcoal grill 4 to 6 inches from medium coals. Cook, turning once, 8 to 10 minutes, or until chicken is done; baste frequently with melted butter.

Help plan an alcohol-free prom or graduation party.

Chicken Nugget Sandwiches

Paula M. Galusha
Free-Lance Home Economist, Tulsa, OK

Chicken nuggets are popular at fast-food restaurants. They can be prepared quickly at home, too. Served in toasted hot dog buns, chicken nuggets make a delicious, different sandwich. Just watch how quickly your family or friends consume these and ask for seconds!

Makes 8 servings

8 chicken breast halves, skinned and boned
Salt and black pepper, to taste
1/3 cup vegetable oil
1 can (8 ounces) tomato sauce
1/3 cup lemon juice

2 tablespoons Worcestershire sauce
1 tablespoon prepared yellow mustard
1 clove garlic, minced
Hot dog buns, toasted

Cut each piece of chicken into 6 to 8 chunks. Thread chicken chunks on metal skewers. Season with salt and pepper.

In a small saucepan, combine oil, tomato sauce, lemon juice, Worcestershire sauce, mustard and garlic; mix well. Bring just to a boil; reduce heat and simmer over low heat 5 minutes. Brush sauce over skewered chicken. Return sauce to heat and let simmer until needed.

Place skewers on gas grill over medium heat or on charcoal grill 4 to 6 inches from medium coals. Cook 4 to 5 minutes; turn and brush with sauce. Cook 2 to 3 minutes, or until chicken is done. Remove chicken from skewers. Serve on toasted hot dog buns. Discard remaining sauce.

Chicken on the Grill

Marion Riedl
Staff Writer, *Ludington Daily News*, Ludington, MI

Camping out and cooking over a wood fire can be challenging when the weather is rainy. If you have dry wood, you can get your fire going and keep it going to develop hot coals for cooking. But you don't want rain dripping on your food if it has to cook very long. In just such a situation, we decided to cube the chicken breasts because cubes would only take about 10 minutes to cook. Now we cook chicken this way almost all the time when we are camping.

Makes 2 servings

1/4 cup vegetable oil
1/4 cup apple, pineapple or
    orange juice
2 tablespoons Worcestershire
    sauce

1 tablespoon lemon juice
1 teaspoon garlic salt
2 chicken breast halves,
    skinned, boned and
    cut into 1-inch cubes

In a large resealable plastic bag, combine oil, apple juice, Worcestershire sauce, lemon juice and garlic salt. Add chicken cubes. Close plastic bag; turn to coat all chicken cubes. Refrigerate (at campsite, put in cooler) 30 to 45 minutes, turning once or twice.

Remove chicken from marinade; discard marinade. Thread chicken cubes on metal skewers. Place skewers on gas grill over medium-high heat or on charcoal grill 8 to 10 inches from medium-hot coals. Cook about 10 minutes, turning occasionally, or until chicken is done.

Tell your legislators that you endorse a .00 blood alcohol content for youth under 21.

Chicken Tenders in Tangy Mustard Sauce

Suzanne Hall
Food Editor, *The Chattanooga Times*, Chattanooga, TN

This appetizer was served at a fund-raising dinner at our city's historic Radisson Read House Hotel. Chicken tenders are simply strips of boneless chicken breast. They are available in most supermarkets or you can save a little money by cutting your own.

Makes 4 servings

12 chicken tenders
2 cups spicy brown mustard
1/2 cup apple juice
1/4 cup lemon juice
Juice of one lime
(about 2 tablespoons)

1 tablespoon ground ginger
1 teaspoon white pepper
1 teaspoon salt

Put chicken pieces in a shallow dish. In a mixing bowl, combine mustard, apple juice, lemon juice, lime juice, ginger, pepper and salt; mix well. Pour 1 cup mustard mixture over chicken; stir to coat chicken. Refrigerate, covered, 20 minutes. Reserve remaining mustard mixture to use as a dipping sauce.

Remove chicken from marinade; discard marinade. Thread chicken onto 4 metal skewers (or wooden skewers that have been soaked in water for 30 minutes).

Place skewers on gas grill over high heat or on charcoal grill about 3 inches from hot coals. Cook 3 to 4 minutes per side, or until chicken is done. Serve chicken tenders as an appetizer, with reserved mustard mixture for dipping.

Chili Relleno Chicken

Beth Whitley Duke
Food Editor, *Amarillo Globe-News*, Amarillo, TX

Jalapeños are the small green peppers that are the trademark of many Tex-Mex recipes. Jalapeños may look as tame as a small green pickle on a plate, but they are full of fire when you bite into them. Chili Relleno — a chili pepper stuffed with cheese, chicken or beef — is a classic Tex-Mex dish. For this grilled version, the chicken is on the outside and the pepper inside. Because most people prefer skinless chicken these days, a piece of bacon around the chicken helps keep it moist. If you are trimming fat from your diet, substitute low-fat cheese and omit the bacon.

Makes 6 servings

6 large chicken breast halves, skinned and boned
6 slices Monterey Jack or Colby cheese

6 jalapeño peppers, fresh or canned (not pickled)
6 slices bacon

Flatten chicken pieces to 1/2-inch thickness by hammering with a kitchen mallet. Place a slice of cheese on each piece of chicken and top each with a jalapeño. Roll chicken around jalapeño. Wrap a slice of bacon around each bundle; secure bacon with a wooden pick that has been soaked in water about 1 hour.

Place chicken bundles on gas grill over high heat or on charcoal grill 4 inches from hot coals. Cook, turning frequently, 35 to 40 minutes, or until done.

Note: To shorten grilling time, precook the chicken bundles in the microwave oven on High (100 percent) power about 10 minutes; complete cooking by grilling chicken 10 to 15 minutes. Or, bake chicken bundles in a preheated 350° oven 20 minutes; complete cooking by grilling chicken 10 to 15 minutes.

You can reduce the heat of the peppers by removing the seeds. Experiment with your family's tastes. You might want to start with half a jalapeño before you turn on the full heat!

Don't let others teach youngsters the wrong lessons about alcohol.

Cilantro Grilled Chicken Breast

Susan Manlin Katzman
Free-Lance Food Writer, St. Louis, MO

In 1987, I wrote an article for FoodStyles *magazine featuring the best brunches in St. Louis. As research, I booked brunches at all of the city's best brunch restaurants. Then I sampled signature specialties in each place in order to find the four best brunch recipes available. (Ah, come on, it's a nasty job, but somebody has to do it.) Tivoli's restaurant won, not only because of the staggering number of different dishes served at brunch but also because of the wonderful quality of each dish. Tivoli's signature dish was Cilantro Grilled Chicken Breast. The restaurant chef shared the recipe, which I printed. Although Tivoli's is no longer, its recipe still graces my table.*

Makes 8 servings

8 chicken breast halves,
   skinned and boned
2 cups olive oil
Juice of 2 lemons
   (about 6 tablespoons)
1/4 cup chopped fresh cilantro
1 teaspoon salt

1 teaspoon ground cumin
1 teaspoon chopped shallots
1/2 teaspoon black pepper
1/4 teaspoon cayenne pepper
2 cloves garlic, minced
1 cup tomato salsa
   (bottled or homemade)

Put chicken in a glass dish large enough to hold chicken pieces in one layer. Combine oil, lemon juice, cilantro, salt, cumin, shallots, pepper, cayenne and garlic. Pour mixture over chicken. Refrigerate, covered, at least 2 hours, turning chicken occasionally.

Remove chicken from marinade, reserving marinade. Put marinade in saucepan and heat to boiling. Reduce heat and let marinade simmer until needed.

Place chicken on oiled rack of gas grill over medium-high heat or on charcoal grill 4 to 6 inches from medium-hot coals. Cook, turning once and basting often with heated marinade, 10 to 20 minutes, or until chicken is firm, opaque and light golden brown. Discard remaining marinade.

Put 2 tablepoons salsa on each serving plate. Put 1 piece chicken on top of salsa. Serve immediately.

Grilled Quail on Toast

Kasey Wilson
Food Columnist, *The Vancouver Courier*, Vancouver, BC, Canada

Quail is no longer a seasonal food that means someone in your house is a good shot. Today quail are raised on game farms. There the birds are fattened up into tender, juicy morsels. These tiny birds cook quickly whether grilled or roasted in the oven.

Makes 4 servings

8 quail, cleaned and split
    lengthwise
Salt and freshly ground black
    pepper, to taste
2 tablespoons Dijon-style mustard
1/4 cup finely chopped fresh herbs,
    such as thyme, rosemary,
    sage or tarragon

Olive oil
8 slices French bread
Butter
Dijon-style mustard
Lemon wedges, for garnish

Rub quail with salt, pepper, 2 tablespoons mustard and herbs. Place quail, skin-side up, on gas grill over medium-high heat or on charcoal grill 4 to 6 inches from medium-hot coals. Cook, covered, 10 to 15 minutes, or until done. Turn occasionally and brush lightly with olive oil during cooking.

Toast bread on grill; spread butter and mustard on each slice. Serve quail on grilled bread. Garnish with lemon wedges.

Tell young people about the dangers of underage drinking.

Greek-Style Kebabs

Mary Beth Jung
Free-Lance Writer, Grafton, WI

Here's a "good-for-you" main dish that's a breeze to prepare and very colorful. If desired, you can marinate the chicken overnight for added flavor and convenience. When squash are in season, thread a few pieces of squash between the chicken and peppers for added color and flavor.

Makes 4 servings

¼ cup olive oil
2 teaspoons lemon juice
1 teaspoon dried oregano
1 clove garlic, minced
1 teaspoon ground cumin
1 tablespoon cracked
    black pepper
1 pound boned and skinned
    chicken breasts, cut into
    1-inch cubes

1 medium-size red bell pepper,
    cut into 1-inch cubes
1 medium-size green bell pepper,
    cut into 1-inch cubes
Steamed rice (optional)

In a shallow dish, combine olive oil, lemon juice, oregano, garlic, cumin and pepper. Add chicken cubes; toss to coat. Refrigerate, covered, 4 to 6 hours, or overnight, turning chicken occasionally.

Thread chicken and red and green pepper cubes alternately on 4 metal skewers. Discard marinade.

Place skewers on gas grill over medium-high heat or on charcoal grill 4 to 6 inches from medium-hot coals. Cook 8 to 10 minutes, turning occasionally, or until chicken is done. Serve over steamed rice, if desired.

Herbed Chicken Breasts

Carolyn Flournoy
Food Columnist, *The Times*, Shreveport, LA

My love of herbs was inspired by one of my mother's friends. She lived several miles from town in a cottage with an herb garden and an assortment of pets (dogs, cats, chickens, rabbits, etc.). I liked to visit her because she always had something wonderful cooking on the stove or her big outdoor barbecue pit. She taught me to use a bunch of herbs tied together for basting, then throw the herbs into the fire to add an extra-special smoke flavor.

Makes 4 servings

4 chicken breast halves,
   skinned and boned
1 tablespoon olive oil
1 tablespoon lemon juice
2 tablespoons chopped
   fresh parsley
2 teaspoons chopped fresh
   lemon thyme

1 teaspoon chopped fresh mint
Salt, to taste
Lemon-pepper seasoning, to taste
1/4 cup mayonnaise
2 teaspoons Dijon-style mustard
4 small poorboy buns or
   French rolls, split

Put chicken breast halves between 2 sheets of waxed paper; pound into thin cutlets. Put chicken in a shallow dish. In a small bowl, combine oil, lemon juice, parsley, lemon thyme, mint, salt and lemon pepper; mix well. Pour herb mixture over chicken; turn pieces to coat well. Refrigerate, covered, 30 to 45 minutes.

Remove chicken from marinade; discard marinade. Place chicken on gas grill over medium-high heat or on charcoal grill 3 to 4 inches from medium-hot coals. Cook 10 to 15 minutes, turning occasionally, or until chicken is done.

Meanwhile, combine mayonnaise and mustard in a small bowl. Spread mayonnaise mixture on buns. Put chicken on buns and serve.

Never serve alcohol to anyone under the age of 21.

Honey-Mustard Chicken

Toni Burks
Free-Lance Writer, Roanoke, VA

Chicken breasts and a punchy brush-on sauce make a winning combination for a quick outdoor supper. This sauce teams two popular flavors — honey and mustard — to give grilled chicken a great taste. For maximum flavor and to prevent burning, brush on the sauce the final few minutes of cooking, when the chicken is done and tender.

Makes 4 servings

2 tablespoons honey	¹/₂ teaspoon poppy seeds
1 tablespoon Dijon-style mustard	¹/₄ teaspoon black pepper
1 tablespoon lemon juice	4 chicken breast halves, skinned

In a small mixing bowl, combine honey, mustard, lemon juice, poppy seeds and pepper; mix well. Set sauce aside.

Rinse chicken pieces with cold running water. Pat dry with paper towels. Place chicken, bone-side up, on gas grill over high heat or on charcoal grill 2 to 3 inches from hot coals. Cook 25 to 30 minutes, turning frequently, or until chicken is done. Brush all surfaces of chicken with reserved sauce. Cook, turning occasionally, 5 minutes, or until nicely browned.

Kebabs with Jalapeño-Honey Sauce

Toni Burks
Free-Lance Writer, Roanoke, VA

Stir-frying isn't the only thing you can do with chicken strips. Try making kebabs by threading chicken strips on skewers and cooking them over glowing coals. A tart, lime-butter marinade ignites a spark of flavor, and a touch of jalapeño pepper in the dipping sauce adds just the right pizzazz.

Makes 4 servings

1/4 cup butter or margarine, melted
2 tablespoons lime juice
1 teaspoon minced fresh garlic
1/4 teaspoon salt
Generous dash freshly ground
    black pepper

1 pound boned and skinned
    chicken breasts, cut into strips
1 small pickled jalapeño pepper
1 cup sour cream
2 tablespoons honey

In a large shallow dish, combine melted butter, lime juice, garlic, salt and pepper; mix well. Add chicken strips; stir to coat well. Refrigerate, covered, at least 1 hour.

Thread chicken strips onto 4 (12-inch) metal skewers. Discard marinade.

Place skewers on gas grill over high heat or on charcoal grill 4 to 6 inches from hot coals. Cook, turning occasionally, 8 to 10 minutes, or until chicken is done and nicely browned.

Meanwhile, trim stem from jalapeño; remove seeds and veins. In container of electric blender or food processor, combine jalapeño, sour cream and honey. Process until smooth. Serve kebabs with jalapeño-honey sauce.

Encourage teenagers to call home for a ride if their driver has been drinking.

Lemon-Herb Chicken Breasts

Clara H. Eschmann
Food Columnist, *The Macon Telegraph*, Macon, GA

Chicken has long been a favorite for my family menus. It is inexpensive, easy to prepare and easy to digest. Consequently, I am always looking for new ways to cook it. One of my readers shared the following recipe, which I find delicious.

Makes 6 servings

1 cup margarine or butter
1/4 cup lemon juice
2 tablespoons grated lemon peel
2 tablespoons finely chopped
   fresh parsley
1 teaspoon dried rosemary
1 teaspoon dried savory

1 teaspoon Worcestershire sauce
1/2 teaspoon dried thyme
3 drops hot pepper sauce
   (optional)
Salt and black pepper, to taste
6 chicken breast halves

In a saucepan, combine margarine, lemon juice, lemon peel, parsley, rosemary, savory, Worcestershire sauce, thyme, hot pepper sauce, salt and pepper; mix well. Cook slowly, stirring, until margarine melts.

Pour lemon-herb marinade into a shallow dish. Place chicken pieces in marinade; spoon marinade over chicken. Let marinate 10 to 15 minutes at room temperature.

Remove chicken from marinade, reserving marinade. Put marinade in saucepan and heat to boiling. Reduce heat and let marinade simmer until needed.

Place chicken, skin-side up, on gas grill over medium-high heat or on charcoal grill about 6 inches from medium-hot coals. Cook 30 to 40 minutes, or until done; turn and baste with heated marinade every 10 minutes. Serve immediately. Discard remaining marinade.

Lemony Herb Chicken

Dorothy Cunningham
Free-Lance Writer, Morenci, MI

Grilled chicken has a delicate flavor all its own, which doesn't come through when it's covered with the usual heavy barbecue sauce. I particularly like chicken with this lemony marinade, and use this recipe often. I especially like to serve it for parties during hot summer weather when light foods are welcome. It goes well with thick tomato slices sprinkled with Parmesan cheese and heated on foil on the grill.

Makes 4 servings

3/4 cup lemon juice
1/4 cup vegetable oil
2 tablespoons finely chopped
　　fresh parsley
2 teaspoons dried dill weed
1 teaspoon salt
1/4 teaspoon freshly ground
　　black pepper

3 pounds chicken parts
　　(or 4 large chicken
　　breast halves)
Lemon slices and fresh parsley
　　sprigs, for garnish

In a shallow dish, combine lemon juice, oil, parsley, dill weed, salt and pepper; mix well. Add chicken pieces; turn to coat. Refrigerate, covered, at least 3 hours, or overnight, turning several times.

Remove chicken from marinade, reserving marinade. Put marinade in saucepan and heat to boiling. Reduce heat and let marinade simmer until needed.

Place chicken on gas grill over high heat or on charcoal grill 6 inches from hot coals. Cook, turning frequently and brushing with heated marinade, 30 to 45 minutes, or until done. Discard remaining marinade.

Serve chicken on platter garnished with lemon slices and fresh parsley sprigs, if desired.

Mexican Chicken

Teri M. Grimes
Features Editor, *The Bradenton Herald*, Bradenton, FL

If you're in the mood for Mexican food but don't want to bother with fajitas or tacos, try grilled chicken — the south-of-the-border way. This method of preparation keeps the chicken moist and tender, and the smoky taste of the meat and the chili peppers are just made for each other. Serve Mexican Chicken with tortillas (which you can throw right on the grill to warm) and baked potatoes (which you can wrap in foil and bake in the coals).

Makes 4 servings

2 serrano chili peppers
2 cloves garlic
Dash ground cloves
Dash ground cinnamon
4 slices bacon, partly cooked

1 roasting chicken
(3½ to 4 pounds)
Cherry tomatoes and additional
serrano chili peppers, for
garnish (optional)

It's a good idea to wear plastic or rubber gloves or put plastic bags over your hands whenever working with hot peppers. Remove stems, seeds and veins from peppers. Finely chop peppers and garlic. Place in a small bowl. Stir in cloves and cinnamon.

Cut bacon into 1-inch pieces.

Lift skin of chicken at neck cavity. Insert hand, lifting skin from meat along breast, thigh and drumstick. Using a small spatula, spread pepper mixture evenly over meat, under the skin. Place a layer of bacon pieces over pepper mixture. Skewer neck skin to back. Tie legs securely to tail and twist wing tips under back of chicken. Insert meat thermometer in center of inside thigh muscle, not touching bone.

In a covered grill, arrange medium-hot charcoal around a drip pan. Place chicken, breast-side up, on grill rack over drip pan. Cover grill; cook 1 hour, or until meat thermometer registers 185°.

If desired, garnish chicken with cherry tomatoes and serrano chili peppers.

Note: To make a drip pan, tear off two sheets of heavy-duty aluminum foil. Double-fold the edges, forming 1½- to 2-inch sides. Score and miter corners for strength.

Make a personal pledge to never drink and drive.

Mushroom-Stuffed Chicken Thighs

Narcisse S. Cadgène
Free-Lance Writer, New York, NY

Moist, meaty and fairly even in shape, boneless chicken thighs are the ideal chicken part for barbecuing. Years ago, I'd have to outmaneuver most of my family to nab a thigh, but today packages of boned thighs are readily available in supermarkets. This revolution in packaging put an end to the domestic scrambling of my youth — unless, of course, there is only one thigh left.

Makes 4 servings

8 large chicken thighs, boned
1 1/2 tablespoons olive oil
1 1/2 cups chopped onions
8 to 10 ounces fresh
   mushrooms, chopped
1 tablespoon minced fresh garlic

1/2 teaspoon salt
1/4 teaspoon freshly ground
   black pepper
2 tablespoons chopped
   fresh cilantro
2 tablespoons soy sauce

Lay the thighs flat, skin-side down, and pound lightly to flatten. Set aside while preparing stuffing.

Heat olive oil in a large skillet. Add onions; sauté over medium-high heat 2 minutes, or until onions are soft. Stir in mushrooms, garlic, salt and pepper. Cook, covered, 3 minutes. Remove cover; cook, stirring constantly, until all visible liquid evaporates. Stir in cilantro. Set aside to cool.

(If you do not plan to cook the chicken within the hour, refrigerate the stuffing and the chicken separately, and continue the recipe just before grilling. If you plan to grill the chicken immediately, you can stuff the thighs while the mushroom mixture is still slightly warm.)

Divide the stuffing into 4 equal portions. Mound one portion in the center of each of 4 chicken thighs. Cover with the remaining thighs, skin-side up. Bring skin of sandwiched thighs together; secure with wooden picks or tie the paired thighs with butcher's twine.

Place on gas grill over medium heat or on charcoal grill 4 to 6 inches from medium coals. Cook about 35 minutes, or until done; turn pieces and baste with soy sauce about every 10 minutes.

Start saying "none for the road" instead of "one for the road."

Mustard Barbecued Chicken

Jim Hillibish
City Editor, *The Repository*, Canton, OH

Tired of tomato-based barbecue sauce? Here's an excellent alternative. Its pungent tang accentuates the smoke flavor from the grill. The honey helps seal in the chicken juices and turns an appetizing caramel color. For a lighter flavor, grill the chicken without the sauce, then brush on the sauce just before serving.

Makes 6 servings

4 pounds chicken pieces
¼ cup white vinegar
½ cup olive oil
¼ cup honey

2 cloves garlic, minced
2 teaspoons dried tarragon
5 tablespoons Dijon-style mustard

Rinse chicken; pat dry with paper towels. In a medium mixing bowl, combine vinegar, olive oil, honey, garlic, tarragon and mustard; mix well. Pour marinade into two (1-quart) resealable plastic bags, dividing equally between bags. Divide chicken evenly between the two bags. Seal bags; turn to coat all chicken pieces. Refrigerate at least 1 hour, turning bags occasionally.

Remove chicken from bags, reserving marinade. Put marinade in saucepan and heat to boiling. Reduce heat and let marinade simmer until needed.

Place chicken on gas grill over medium heat or on charcoal grill 4 to 6 inches from medium coals. Cook chicken, turning at least once and basting frequently with heated marinade, 35 to 45 minutes, or until done. Discard remaining marinade.

Spicy Lemon Chicken

Barbara Burklo
Food Editor (Retired), *Santa Cruz Sentinel*, Soquel, CA

The youth director at our church, Laura Hamby, often presides at the barbecue grill when her youth group sponsors fund-raising dinners. Her specialty is chicken, and fresh lemon juice is her key to flavor. This method works equally well whether you are cooking for a crowd or just a few people.

Makes 4 servings

4 chicken breast halves, skinned and boned
4 (or more) large lemons
2 tablespoons bottled Italian-style oil and vinegar salad dressing
2 tablespoons bottled barbecue sauce
2 dashes hot pepper sauce
2 dashes Worcestershire sauce
Salt and black pepper, to taste

The day before cooking, place chicken pieces in a shallow dish; squeeze enough fresh lemon juice to completely cover chicken. Refrigerate, covered, overnight, turning chicken occasionally.

Remove chicken from lemon juice. To the lemon juice, add Italian dressing, barbecue sauce, hot pepper sauce, Worcestershire sauce, salt and pepper; mix well. Dip each chicken piece in mixture. Immediately place chicken on gas grill over high heat or on charcoal grill 4 to 6 inches from hot coals. Brush lemon mixture on top of each piece; discard remaining mixture. Cook, turning several times, 10 to 20 minutes, or until chicken is done.

Please say, "Yes" the next time a MADD volunteer asks for your support.

Turkey Burgers

Caroline Stuart
Cookbook Author, Greenwich, CT

In recent years, a welcome addition to supermarket meat sections is the availability of turkey parts, even when it isn't holiday time. I especially like to use ground turkey instead of ground beef to make burgers for the grill. You also can make chicken burgers by cutting the meat off the bone and putting it through a meat grinder or chopping it in a food processor.

Makes 4 servings

1 pound ground turkey
1/4 cup chopped onion or
  green onions
1/4 cup shredded Cheddar or
  Swiss cheese
2 teaspoons dried thyme or
  oregano

2 teaspoons Worcestershire sauce
Hot pepper sauce, to taste
Salt and freshly ground black
  pepper, to taste
4 slices bacon (optional)
4 hamburger buns

Shape ground turkey into 8 thin patties. Sprinkle equal portions of onion, cheese, thyme, Worcestershire sauce, hot pepper sauce, salt and pepper over half of the patties. Cover seasoned patties with the remaining patties; press the edges to seal. Wrap a slice of bacon around the outside edge of each burger and secure with a wooden pick.

Place on gas grill over medium-high heat or on charcoal grill 4 to 6 inches from medium-hot coals. Cook about 4 to 6 minutes per side, or until done.

To toast the buns, place buns, cut-side down, on the edge of the grill for a few minutes. Serve burgers on toasted buns, with condiments of choice.

Virgin Islands Grilled Turkey

Jim Hillibish
City Editor, *The Repository*, Canton, OH

Exotic flavors of peanut, ginger and nutmeg combine in this Caribbean turkey grill. Be sure to use breast meat with skin because the skin helps to lock in the juices. Looking for some way to serve turkey other than hot? Let it cool, slice it and use it to top a salad of fresh greens, orange slices and shredded coconut, with your favorite sweet-and-sour dressing.

Makes 4 to 6 servings

1 whole turkey breast, boned, with skin on	2 tablespoons cider vinegar
3/4 cup chunky peanut butter	3 teaspoons ground ginger
1/2 cup soy sauce	3 teaspoons dried basil
1/4 cup lime juice	2 cloves garlic, minced
1/4 cup olive oil	1 teaspoon ground nutmeg
	1 teaspoon crushed red pepper

Thaw turkey, if frozen. Rinse turkey; pat dry with paper towels. Put turkey in a shallow dish.

In container of electric blender or food processor, combine peanut butter, soy sauce, lime juice, olive oil, vinegar, ginger, basil, garlic, nutmeg and red pepper flakes; blend until smooth. Pour half of the peanut butter sauce over turkey; spoon sauce over turkey to coat. Refrigerate turkey, covered, at least 2 hours, or overnight.

Refrigerate remaining peanut butter sauce in a separate covered container. (This will be used for basting turkey.)

Remove turkey from marinade; discard marinade. Place turkey on gas grill over medium-high heat or charcoal grill over medium-hot coals. Cook, covered, until meat thermometer reaches 170°, basting frequently with remaining peanut butter sauce. (Allow 11 to 15 minutes per pound.) Let turkey stand 10 minutes before carving.

Note: You can substitute chicken breasts for turkey.

FISH & SEAFOOD

70   Bacon-Wrapped Shrimp

71   California-Style Fish in Lettuce Wraps

72   Chili Shrimp

73   Clams and Mussels in their Shells

74   Grilled Fish with Herbs

75   Grilled Fish Sandwich

76   Grilled Salmon

77   Halibut with Thyme

78   Hawaiian Grilled Swordfish with Papaya

79   Lemon-Dill Scallops

80   Mahi-Mahi in Ti Leaves

81   Mahi-Mahi with Caesar Sauce

82   Mussels with Curry Butter

83   Oyster Pan Roast

84   Seafood Boats

85   Seafood-Citrus Kebabs

86   Snappy Snapper

87   Softshell Crabs on the Grill

88   Swordfish on the Grill

89   Tangy Grilled Shrimp

90   Tarragon Grilled Salmon

Bacon-Wrapped Shrimp

Teri M. Grimes
Features Editor, *The Bradenton Herald*, Bradenton, FL

In Florida, fresh shrimp are so plentiful that we are always looking for new ways to prepare them. These bacon-wrapped shrimp form the basis for a great meal. Serve them with rice and grilled zucchini.

Makes 6 servings

1 pound fresh or frozen shrimp,
   shelled and deveined
   (use medium or large shrimp)
1 small onion, finely chopped
1/2 cup olive oil
1/2 teaspoon garlic powder

1/2 teaspoon granulated sugar
1/2 teaspoon cayenne pepper
1/4 teaspoon salt
1/4 teaspoon dried oregano
1/2 pound bacon

Thaw shrimp, if frozen.

In a small mixing bowl, combine onion, olive oil, garlic powder, sugar, cayenne, salt and oregano; mix well. Place the shrimp in a resealable plastic bag; place bag in a deep bowl. Pour marinade over shrimp; close bag. Turn bag several times to coat shrimp. Refrigerate shrimp 3 hours, turning bag occasionally.

Halve bacon slices lengthwise and crosswise. In a large skillet, partly cook the bacon. Drain on paper towels.

Drain shrimp; discard marinade. Wrap bacon slices around shrimp; secure with wooden picks. Place shrimp in a wire grill basket or on a large piece of heavy-duty aluminum foil. If using foil, puncture the foil in several places.

Place grill basket or foil on gas grill over medium-high heat or on charcoal grill 4 to 6 inches from medium-hot coals. Cook 8 to 10 minutes, or until bacon and shrimp are done, turning basket or individual shrimp once. Serve immediately.

Ask bars, restaurants and arenas to sponsor Designated Driver programs.

California-Style Fish in Lettuce Wraps

Jeanne Voltz
Cookbook Author, Pittsboro, NC

One evening we discovered that a lettuce or cabbage leaf wrapped loosely around fish eliminates sticking to the grill. The greens are charred, but the fish is juicy and full of flavor. The orange sauce brings out the best in many fish varieties.

Makes 4 to 6 servings

2 pounds fish fillets
   (snapper, rock cod,
   monkfish, sea bass, etc.)
3/4 cup orange juice
1/4 cup vegetable oil
2 teaspoons soy sauce
1 teaspoon grated orange peel

1/2 teaspoon finely chopped
   fresh ginger
1/4 teaspoon freshly ground
   black pepper
2 cloves garlic, minced
6 to 8 large lettuce leaves
Lemon wedges

Place fish in a shallow dish. In a small bowl, combine orange juice, oil, soy sauce, orange peel, ginger, pepper and garlic; mix well. Pour orange juice mixture over fish. Cover and marinate 30 minutes at room temperature or up to 2 hours in the refrigerator.

Drain fish, discarding marinade. Loosely wrap each fish fillet in a lettuce leaf, tucking in edges.

Oil the grill rack. Place lettuce-wrapped fish on gas grill over high heat or on charcoal grill 4 to 5 inches from hot coals. Cook, turning occasionally, 12 to 15 minutes, or until fish is done. Peel off lettuce, which will be charred, and discard it. Serve fish hot with lemon wedges.

Chili Shrimp

Mary D. Scourtes
Food Writer, *The Tampa Tribune*, Tampa, FL

The reality of rushing home from work and cooking dinner when you would rather be cooling off in the pool makes dinner time during prime heat time seem like drudgery. Shrimp, however, are quick and easy to prepare on the grill. Serve these spicy shrimp with rice, bread and a mixed green salad for dinner in a flash.

Makes 6 servings

1/2 cup finely chopped fresh parsley	1 tablespoon grated fresh ginger
1/3 cup white wine vinegar	1 teaspoon black pepper
1/3 cup chili sauce	1 clove garlic, minced
2 tablespoons Worcestershire sauce	1/8 teaspoon hot pepper sauce
2 tablespoons vegetable oil	2 pounds medium shrimp, shelled and deveined

In a large bowl, combine parsley, vinegar, chili sauce, Worcestershire sauce, oil, ginger, pepper, garlic and hot pepper sauce; mix well. Add shrimp; stir to evenly coat shrimp. Refrigerate, covered, 2 hours.

Drain shrimp, discarding marinade. Thread shrimp on 6 metal skewers, aligning shrimp so they lie flat. Place skewers on well-oiled rack on gas grill over medium heat or on charcoal grill 4 to 6 inches from medium coals. Cook, turning once, 6 to 8 minutes, or until shrimp are pink and opaque throughout.

Select a Designated Driver when your outing will involve alcohol.

Clams and Mussels in their Shells

Narcisse S. Cadgène
Free-Lance Writer, New York, NY

Appetizers, anyone? Grilling shellfish is a trick we use to ensure plenty of company at the grill, especially when we're cooking a main course that takes a long time, such as ribs. Because shellfish only take a few minutes to open, cook them "to order," a few at a time if necessary, while the recipient chats with the chef.

Makes 6 servings

12 cherrystone or littleneck clams, in the shell
12 large mussels, in the shell (preferably farm-raised)
$1/2$ cup white vinegar
$1/4$ cup lemon juice
$1/4$ cup water

1 tablespoon finely chopped fresh parsley
1 tablespoon finely chopped onion
1 tablespoon finely chopped red bell pepper
Few drops hot pepper sauce

Scrub the clams until free of grit. Clean the mussels by pulling off the hairy beard and scrubbing the shells well with a stiff brush; farm-raised mussels will have little or no beard. Rinse clams and mussels in cold running water; discard any that do not stay tightly closed while being handled. Refrigerate shellfish until cooking time.

In a small bowl, combine vinegar, lemon juice, water, parsley, onion, bell pepper and hot pepper sauce; mix well. Set sauce aside.

Place clams and mussels, heavy hinge-side down, on a gas grill over high heat or on a charcoal grill over hot coals. Cook mussels 2 or 3 minutes, clams 5 minutes, or until the shells open. Using a long-handled spoon or tongs, carefully move the opened shellfish from the grill, saving any liquid which collects in the shell. Discard any that do not open.

Spoon about $1/2$ teaspoon sauce onto each clam or mussel. Eat directly from the shell.

Grilled Fish with Herbs

Jane Gray
Food Editor, *Ludington Daily News*, Ludington, MI

One of the perks of being the food editor of the local newspaper is the opportunity to try recipes submitted by the readers. When we featured this recipe in a story about grilling, it triggered a lot of favorable reader response. Many readers mentioned the easy preparation and quick clean-up.

Makes 4 servings

4 fish steaks (any type), 6 to 8 ounces each	1/2 teaspoon dried basil
2 1/2 tablespoons lemon juice	1/2 teaspoon dried parsley
2 tablespoons butter or margarine, melted	1/2 teaspoon dried thyme
	Hot pepper sauce, to taste
	Salt and black pepper, to taste

Place each fish steak on separate piece of heavy-duty aluminum foil. In a small bowl, combine lemon juice, butter, basil, parsley and thyme; mix well. Pour equal amount of mixture over each fish steak. Sprinkle 1 to 2 drops hot pepper sauce on each fish steak, if desired. Season fish with salt and pepper. Wrap fish securely in foil.

Place foil packets on gas grill over high heat or on charcoal grill 4 to 6 inches from hot coals. Cook 7 to 10 minutes, or until fish flakes easily when tested with a fork.

Never let friends or relatives drink and drive.

Grilled Fish Sandwich

Susan Manlin Katzman
Free-Lance Food Writer, St. Louis, MO

Just about the easiest item to grill is fish and this is just about the easiest grilled fish recipe I have. I developed the recipe for a hamburger-loving friend who was told to cut down on beef. He liked to grill, but said that he didn't like the taste of fish. Wrong! We served the fish just the way he likes his burgers (with mayonnaise, tomato, lettuce and onion) and he was hooked. Now he cooks all sorts of fish on the grill, but I think this sandwich remains his favorite.

Makes 1 serving

1 boneless fish steak (shark, tuna or swordfish)	Sliced tomato
	Lettuce
Mayonnaise	Sliced red onion (optional)
Kaiser roll or hamburger bun	

Coat both sides of fish steak with mayonnaise. Place fish on oiled rack of gas grill over medium-high heat or on charcoal grill 4 to 6 inches from medium-hot coals. Cook fish 5 to 6 minutes, or until fish is light golden brown on underside. Turn fish and continue cooking until fish is just cooked through. Do not overcook. (As a general rule, measure fish at thickest part and cook 10 minutes per inch of thickness, turning once.) Serve on a Kaiser roll or hamburger bun with tomato, lettuce, onion and additional mayonnaise.

Grilled Salmon

Laura Barton
Free-Lance Writer, Portland, OR

The Northwest is known for salmon, and rightfully so. We are lucky to have friends who are enthusiastic salmon fishermen but who don't like to eat salmon. We are always happy to take some off their hands and we fire up the barbecue grill as soon as our friends call. This simple marinade keeps the fish moist without overwhelming the wonderful fresh salmon flavor.

Makes 4 to 5 servings

4 to 5 large salmon fillets
   (3/4 to 1 pound each)
1/4 cup vegetable oil
3 tablespoons soy sauce

2 tablespoons lemon juice
1 large clove garlic, minced
1/2 teaspoon dried thyme or sage

Place salmon fillets in a shallow dish. In a small mixing bowl, combine oil, soy sauce, lemon juice, garlic and thyme; mix well. Pour over salmon. Refrigerate, covered, 1 hour, turning salmon occasionally.

Cover the grill rack with aluminum foil, or use a fine-mesh fish/vegetable grill basket. Remove salmon from marinade, reserving marinade. Put marinade in saucepan and heat to boiling. Reduce heat and let simmer until needed.

Place salmon, skin-side down, on gas grill over medium heat or on charcoal grill 4 to 6 inches from medium-hot coals. Cook, turning occasionally and basting with heated marinade, 20 to 25 minutes, or until salmon flakes easily when tested with a fork. Discard remaining marinade.

Volunteer to help the MADD chapter nearest you.

Halibut with Thyme

Jane Baker
Free-Lance Writer, East Lansing, MI

I like to grill fish on Friday night. It's a quick and easy meal on a night when I especially enjoy relaxing. I often purchase halibut steaks on the way home from work, marinate them briefly, then grill them. My favorite accompaniment for grilled halibut is tomato salsa. Its spicy flavor accents the fish without overpowering it.

Makes 4 servings

4 fresh or frozen halibut
   steaks, 1-inch thick
   (about 6 ounces each)
1/3 cup olive oil
1/3 cup chicken broth

3 green onions, sliced
2 cloves garlic, minced
1 teaspoon dried thyme
1/4 teaspoon lemon-pepper
   seasoning

Thaw halibut, if frozen. Place halibut in a shallow dish. In a small mixing bowl, combine olive oil, broth, green onions, garlic, thyme and lemon pepper; mix well. Pour oil mixture over fish. Marinate about 30 minutes at room temperature or refrigerate, covered, 1 to 2 hours.

Remove fish from marinade, reserving marinade. Put marinade in saucepan and heat to boiling. Reduce heat and let simmer until needed.

Place fish on gas grill over medium heat or on charcoal grill 4 to 6 inches from medium coals. Cook, turning once and basting with heated marinade, 8 to 12 minutes, or until fish flakes easily when tested with a fork. Serve immediately. Discard remaining marinade.

Hawaiian Grilled Swordfish with Papaya

Barbara Fisher
Food Writer, *This Week Publications*, Farmingdale, NY

Here's something invitingly tropical: swordfish steaks, grilled Hawaiian style. It's "no ka oi" (the best)! Marinate the fish in a pineapple sauce seasoned with cayenne and cumin and top it with grilled papaya slices. If desired, cover the grill to infuse the fish with a delicious smoky flavor. Serve the swordfish with a piquant rice or pasta dish.

Makes 4 servings

4 swordfish steaks, 1-inch thick
1/2 cup pineapple juice
2 tablespoons lemon juice
1/2 teaspoon cayenne pepper
1/2 teaspoon ground cumin
1/2 teaspoon salt
1 clove garlic, minced

1 tablespoon olive oil
1/2 cup crushed pineapple
1 ripe papaya, peeled
2 tablespoons butter or
    margarine, melted
1/2 teaspoon ground nutmeg

Place swordfish in a shallow dish. In a medium mixing bowl, combine pineapple juice, lemon juice, cayenne, cumin, salt, garlic and olive oil; mix well. Stir in crushed pineapple. Pour pineapple mixture over swordfish. Refrigerate, covered, 15 to 30 minutes, turning fish occasionally.

Remove fish from marinade, reserving marinade. Let fish stand for a few minutes at room temperature. Meanwhile, put marinade in saucepan and heat to boiling. Reduce heat and let marinade simmer until needed.

Place fish on oiled rack on gas grill over high heat or on charcoal grill 5 to 7 inches from hot coals. Cook, turning once and brushing with heated marinade, about 10 minutes, or until fish is just opaque in the center and flakes when tested with a fork. Discard remaining marinade.

Meanwhile, cut papaya crosswise into circular slices about 1-inch thick; remove and discard seeds. Place slices in a foil tray. Drizzle with butter and garnish with nutmeg. Set tray on grill for last 3 minutes of fish cooking time, or until papaya is hot.

Serve fish topped with papaya slices.

Support your local MADD chapter.

Lemon-Dill Scallops

Clara H. Eschmann
Food Columnist, *The Macon Telegraph*, Macon, GA

On a Baltic Sea cruise in late August 1993, I was delighted to find that the cruise line offered heart-healthy choices at each meal. The ship's executive chef shared some of his recipes, including this light recipe that is a particular favorite of mine. It's especially good served with steamed fresh asparagus.

Makes 1 serving

6 sea scallops
(about 6 ounces total)
5 cherry tomatoes, rinsed
and drained
5 small pickled onions
1 1/2 tablespoons fresh lemon juice

1 tablespoon chopped fresh dill
1 tablespoon margarine, melted
1 clove garlic, minced
Paprika, lemon wedges and fresh
dill sprigs, for garnish

Pick over scallops for any pieces of shell that might be still clinging. Rinse scallops; pat dry with paper towels. Skewer scallops on a 10- to 12-inch metal skewer, placing a tomato and an onion between each scallop; begin and end with a scallop.

In a small bowl, combine lemon juice, dill, margarine and garlic; mix well. Brush sauce over scallops and vegetables on skewer, coating well.

Place skewer on gas grill over medium heat or on charcoal grill 4 to 6 inches from medium-hot coals. Cook 5 minutes. Brush with remaining sauce and turn skewer. Cook 5 to 6 minutes, or until tomatoes are soft and scallops are done. Garnish with paprika, lemon wedges and dill sprigs.

Mahi-Mahi in Ti Leaves

Jeanne Voltz
Cookbook Author, Pittsboro, NC

The meaty texture and mild flavor of mahi-mahi make it everybody's favorite fish. This preparation evokes a Pacific beach, the surf rolling in and palm fronds rustling in the breeze. The recipe is modeled after the roasted fish offered at beach parties. Ti leaves are available from florists, but make sure they have not been sprayed. If ti leaves are not to be found, use green corn husks soaked in ice water, or, if all else fails, fresh cabbage or lettuce leaves.

Makes 4 to 6 servings

Ti leaves
1½ pounds mahi-mahi fillets
1 to 2 teaspoons coarse salt
3 tablespoons chopped bacon or
　　salt pork

3 tablespoons finely chopped
　　Maui or other sweet onion
1 bay leaf, crumbled

Spread ti leaves on a table, overlapping them to form a solid wrapper. Make four to six wrappers. Divide the fish between the wrappers. Rub fillets with salt; top each fillet with some of the bacon, onion and bay leaf. Wrap the leaves firmly around the fish; tie packets with a stem stripped from a leaf or with twine.

Place leaf packets on gas grill over high heat or on charcoal grill 3 to 4 inches from hot coals. Cook, turning two or three times, 20 to 25 minutes, or until fish is opaque but still moist at the thickest parts when tested with the tip of a knife pushed through the leaf packet.

Serve hot, opening the packets on fresh ti leaves or shredded greens at the table.

　Attend a MADD event and discover why your support is so important.

Mahi-Mahi with Caesar Sauce

Mary D. Scourtes
Food Writer, *The Tampa Tribune*, Tampa, FL

Haste makes waste when cooking fish and seafood. Don't rush to put the seafood on the grill before the coals are covered with a light ash and are no longer flaming. Caesar salad fans will like this tangy basting sauce made with garlic, lemon and anchovies.

Makes 4 servings

1/4 cup butter or margarine
Juice of 2 lemons
  (about 6 tablespoons)
2 cloves garlic, minced
2 anchovies, mashed

2 tablespoons finely chopped
  fresh parsley
1 teaspoon cracked black pepper
4 mahi-mahi fillets
  (4 to 6 ounces each)

Melt butter in a small saucepan. Add lemon juice, garlic, anchovies, parsley and pepper. Cook, stirring occasionally, over low heat 10 minutes. Let simmer until needed.

Place fish on gas grill over medium heat or on charcoal grill 4 to 6 inches from medium coals. Cook, turning once and basting often with anchovy mixture, 7 to 10 minutes, or until fish flakes easily when tested with a fork. Discard remaining anchovy mixture.

Mussels with Curry Butter

Teri M. Grimes
Features Editor, *The Bradenton Herald*, Bradenton, FL

I only recently discovered the pleasures of mussels. I first tasted them in Baltimore, but had rarely seen them in Florida except on seafood buffets at my favorite restaurants. With the availability of farm-raised mussels, I can now enjoy these tasty morsels any time. They come packaged in 2-pound bags in the seafood departments of most supermarkets. One advantage of farm-raised mussels is that they do not have to be soaked to remove sand. This grill presentation is a snap to prepare and preserves the best part about eating mussels — sopping up the delicious juices.

Makes 4 servings

2 pounds mussels, in the shell
3 tablespoons butter, softened
2 cloves garlic, pressed
1 teaspoon curry powder
1/2 teaspoon ground cumin
1/8 teaspoon salt

1 large lime
1 cup diced red bell pepper
1/4 cup finely chopped
   fresh parsley
French bread

Clean the mussels by pulling off the beards (the dark threads that look a bit like seaweed) and scrubbing the shells well with a stiff brush. Rinse in cold running water; discard any that do not stay tightly closed while being handled. Refrigerate until cooking time.

In a small mixing bowl, combine butter, garlic, curry powder, cumin and salt; mix well. Set aside.

Cut the lime in half crosswise; cut one half into thin slices and the other half into 4 wedges.

Divide mussels evenly among 4 large sheets of aluminum foil; spread mussels into a single layer. Dot mussels with reserved curry butter; scatter bell pepper, parsley and lime slices over mussels. Loosely close the foil to make 4 packets.

Place the foil packets on gas grill over medium-high heat or on charcoal grill 4 to 6 inches from medium-hot coals. Cook 5 to 10 minutes, or until the mussels have opened. Discard any mussels that do not open. Serve with lime wedges and plenty of French bread to soak up the juices.

Get involved today in the anti-drunk driving movement.

Oyster Pan Roast

Jeanne Voltz
Cookbook Author, Pittsboro, NC

In a pan roast, oysters are plumped quickly in butter and seasoned deftly for a quick, light supper. They are a specialty of Grand Central Oyster Bar in New York City, where the oysters are flash-cooked in copper pans over a gas flame. But that doesn't hold the romance of oysters sizzling in butter over a beach fire. This amount is just right for two. Do them in batches for four or six diners.

Makes 2 servings

3 tablespoons butter
1 pint oysters, partly drained
4 slices bread
Butter, for bread
1 tablespoon chopped
    fresh parsley

1/2 teaspoon Worcestershire sauce
1/4 teaspoon salt
1/4 teaspoon freshly ground
    black pepper
1/4 teaspoon paprika

Light fire on the beach or in a charcoal grill 20 to 30 minutes before cooking to allow it to burn down to hot coals. Place 3 tablespoons butter in a shallow skillet. Set skillet on gas grill over high heat or on charcoal grill or over beach fire 4 to 6 inches from hot coals. Cook until butter is melted and sizzling. Add oysters; cook 4 to 5 minutes, or until the edges curl and the oysters are plumped.

While the oysters are cooking, toast the bread in a hinged rack or on a long fork over the fire; butter the toast.

Add parsley, Worcestershire sauce, salt, pepper and paprika to oysters in skillet; stir. Spoon oysters and juices onto buttered toast. Serve immediately.

Seafood Boats

Debra Carr-Elsing
Food Writer, *The Capital Times*, Madison, WI

When a backyard barbecue calls for something a little different and more festive than hot dogs and hamburgers, try this idea for a knock-out entrée. Split fresh pineapples in half, hollow them to form boats, then grill them until lightly browned. Assemble kebabs of shrimp, scallops, green pepper and pineapple and baste them with a snappy glaze. Fill warmed pineapple boats with a hot rice and green onion mixture, then top them with the kebabs.

Makes 4 servings

2 medium pineapples
1 cup bottled red Russian
   salad dressing
1/3 cup firmly packed brown sugar
1/2 teaspoon ground ginger
1/2 pound shrimp, peeled
   and deveined

1/2 pound sea scallops
1 large green bell pepper, cut
   into chunks
2 cups hot cooked rice
3 tablespoons chopped
   green onions

Cut pineapples in half lengthwise. Cut fruit from the shells. Set shells aside. Cut the pineapple into chunks.

In a small bowl, combine salad dressing, brown sugar and ginger; mix well.

Rinse shrimp and scallops; pat dry with paper towels. Alternately thread shrimp, scallops, bell pepper and pineapple chunks on 4 metal skewers.

Place kebabs on gas grill over medium heat or on charcoal grill 5 to 7 inches from medium coals. Cook 10 to 15 minutes, or until seafood is done; turn kebabs and baste frequently with dressing mixture.

Meanwhile, wrap leaves of pineapple shells in aluminum foil. Place shells, cut-side down, on grill alongside kebabs. Cook 8 to 10 minutes, or until shells are lightly brown. Remove from grill and remove foil.

Combine rice and green onions; spoon mixture into grilled pine-apple shells. Place kebabs on top of rice. Serve immediately. Discard remaining dressing mixture.

Seafood-Citrus Kebabs

Jim Hillibish
City Editor, *The Repository*, Canton, OH

These kebabs bring a splash of color to your table. Shellfish seem to be made for skewering and grilling. The subtle shellfish flavors plus the smoke and citrus result in an unusual seafood main course. Serve the kebabs with rice for a super meal in no time.

Makes 4 servings

1 pound large shrimp, peeled and deveined	1 grapefruit
	1 cup tomato sauce
1 pound sea scallops	2 tablespoons honey
1 pound fresh mushrooms	2 tablespoons cider vinegar
1 red bell pepper	2 tablespoons butter or margarine
1 yellow bell pepper	1 tablespoon Worcestershire sauce
2 medium oranges	1 tablespoon soy sauce

Rinse shrimp and scallops in cold water; drain well. Rinse mushrooms; drain well, then cut into thick slices. Remove seeds from red and yellow bell peppers; cut into large chunks. Peel, seed and section oranges and grapefruit.

Skewer shrimp, scallops, mushrooms, bell peppers, orange sections and grapefruit sections alternately on 4 long metal skewers.

In a small saucepan, combine tomato sauce, honey, vinegar, butter, Worcestershire sauce and soy sauce; mix well. Simmer 10 minutes over low heat. Baste kebabs with sauce.

Place kebabs on gas grill over medium heat or charcoal grill 4 to 6 inches from medium coals. Cook 6 to 10 minutes, or until the shrimp turn pink. For a more smoky flavor, cover the grill. Turn kebabs at least once and, if desired, baste again with sauce.

Bring remaining sauce to a boil: simmer 5 minutes, stirring often. Serve as a dipping sauce with kebabs.

Snappy Snapper

Mary D. Scourtes
Food Writer, *The Tampa Tribune*, Tampa, FL

One must choose the proper attire for cooking outdoors. While the traditional chef's hat and apron seem appropriate for most cooks in my neighborhood, my husband prefers clothes that camouflage any dripping barbecue sauce. Just about any fish fillet becomes the perfect foundation for a special dinner when it is teamed with the flavor of outdoor cooking.

Makes 4 servings

1/2 cup low-fat mayonnaise
1/4 cup coarse-grain mustard
1 tablespoon minced fresh garlic
2 tablespoons fresh lime juice
1 tablespoon hot pepper sauce

2 tablespoons finely chopped
   fresh parsley
4 fillets (4 ounces each) snapper,
   bass or other firm fish

In a small bowl, combine mayonnaise, mustard, garlic, lime juice and hot pepper sauce; mix well. Measure 1/4 cup mayonnaise mixture and stir in parsley; refrigerate until needed.

Rinse fish; pat dry with paper towels. Coat both sides of fillets with remaining mayonnaise mixture. Refrigerate, covered, 30 minutes, or overnight.

Place fish on gas grill over medium-high heat or charcoal grill 4 to 6 inches from medium-hot coals. Cook 4 to 5 minutes on each side, basting with reserved mayonnaise-parsley mixture, or until fish is done. Serve immediately. Discard remaining mayonnaise-parsley mixture.

Never serve alcohol to anyone who has had too much to drink.

Softshell Crabs on the Grill

Beth W. Orenstein
Free-Lance Writer, Northampton, PA

Softshell crabs, only in season from mid-May through mid-August, are one of my favorite seafood treats. The traditional ways to cook them are sautéing or deep frying, but we tried grilling them and thought they were absolutely delicious. Now that's the only way we cook them. The tartar sauce is optional. The crabs are so good, you might prefer them plain.

Makes 2 to 4 servings

1/2 cup mayonnaise
2 tablespoons sweet pickle relish
1/2 teaspoon Worcestershire sauce
Salt and black pepper, to taste

2 tablespoons butter, melted
2 tablespoons lemon juice
4 softshell crabs, cleaned

In a small bowl, combine mayonnaise, pickle relish, Worcestershire sauce, salt and pepper. Refrigerate tartar sauce, covered, until serving time.

In a small bowl, combine butter and lemon juice; mix well.

Rinse crabs thoroughly; pat dry with paper towels. Place crabs on gas grill over high heat or on charcoal grill 4 to 6 inches from hot coals. Cook 7 to 9 minutes per side, or until done; baste often with butter mixture.

Serve crabs warm with chilled tartar sauce.

Swordfish on the Grill

Carolyn Flournoy
Food Columnist, *The Times*, Shreveport, LA

With the health-minded '90s, everyone is counting grams and milligrams of fat, cholesterol and sodium in addition to the number of calories and the percentage of calories from fat. Taking a tip from our family doctor, we've been eating a lot of fish. Of course, we used to fry fish but that's out, so I've discovered one of the best ways of preparing it is on the grill. The secret here is to not overcook fish; grill it just until it flakes easily.

Makes 4 servings

2 tablespoons grated lemon peel
2 tablespoons chopped fresh basil
  (or 2 teaspoons dried)
3 tablespoons olive oil

2 cloves garlic, minced
4 swordfish steaks, 1-inch thick
Salt and seasoned pepper, to taste

In a shallow dish, combine lemon peel, basil, olive oil and garlic. Add swordfish. Season with salt and seasoned pepper. Turn steaks to coat with marinade. Refrigerate, covered, 1 hour.

Brush grill rack with olive oil or spray with nonstick cooking spray. Remove swordfish from marinade, reserving marinade. Put marinade in saucepan and heat to boiling. Reduce heat and let marinade simmer until needed.

Place swordfish on gas grill over medium-high heat or on charcoal grill 3 to 4 inches from medium-hot coals. Cook 5 to 6 minutes, or until lightly browned. With a wide spatula, carefully turn steaks. Spoon some heated marinade over fish. Cook until second side browns and fish flakes easily when tested with a fork. Discard remaining marinade.

Don't serve alcohol to guests who have already had too much to drink.

Tangy Grilled Shrimp

Marion Riedl
Staff Writer, *Ludington Daily News*, Ludington, MI

We like to try different foods when we go camping. This recipe, although not the usual camp fare, is a welcome change from beef and chicken and is relatively simple and quick to prepare. Purchase frozen large shrimp in the shell, and cook them for your first camp meal because it is difficult to keep foods frozen in a cooler. They should be almost thawed by the time you get to camp and get your fire built.

Makes 4 servings

1 can (16 ounces) unsweetened
    pineapple chunks
1/2 cup vegetable oil
1 tablespoon Worcestershire
    sauce

1 pound frozen large shrimp in
    the shell, thawed

Drain pineapple, reserving 1/4 cup juice. In a small bowl, combine reserved 1/4 cup pineapple juice, oil and Worcestershire sauce; mix well.

Peel shrimp. Thread shrimp and pineapple chunks alternately on metal skewers. Place skewers on gas grill over medium heat, on charcoal grill 4 to 6 inches from medium coals, or over wood fire 8 to 10 inches from coals. Baste skewers with sauce. Cook 8 to 10 minutes, turning often and basting with sauce each time, or until shrimp are pink. Serve immediately. Discard remaining sauce.

Tarragon Grilled Salmon

Eleanor Ostman
Food Writer, *St. Paul Pioneer Press*, St. Paul, MN

Minnesota is nowhere near an ocean, but it has salmon farms. Former iron ore mining pits on the Iron Range, where I was born, now are filled with crystal clear water and are home to a growing salmon farming industry. I'm always looking for new recipes to showcase this superb fish, and this one is a favorite because it uses my herb of preference, tarragon. It's especially good with buttered spinach pasta and braised cherry tomatoes.

Makes 4 servings

4 salmon fillets (about 6 ounces each)	1 cup clam juice
2 tablespoons olive oil	1 shallot, finely chopped
2 tablespoons minced fresh tarragon, divided	$1/2$ cup heavy cream
1 cup vegetable broth	Salt and white pepper, to taste
	$1/4$ cup cold butter, cut into pats
	Fresh tarragon leaves, for garnish

Rub salmon fillets with olive oil. Sprinkle 1 tablespoon tarragon over salmon and pat into oil. Refrigerate, covered, until ready to cook.

In a large skillet, combine vegetable broth, clam juice, shallot and remaining 1 tablespoon tarragon. Bring to a boil; cook about 10 minutes, or until mixture is reduced to about 3/4 cup. Reduce heat; add cream. Cook over low heat about 5 minutes, or until sauce thickens. Strain sauce. Season with salt and pepper. Keep sauce warm while grilling salmon.

Place salmon, skin-side down, on oiled rack of a gas grill over medium heat or on charcoal grill 4 to 6 inches from medium-hot coals. Cook, turning once, 10 to 12 minutes, or until salmon is just opaque at center.

Swirl cold butter into warm sauce until just melted. Place salmon on a serving platter or individual plates; pour sauce over salmon. Garnish with tarragon leaves, if desired.

Be a responsible guest. Don't drink to excess at your host's home.

VEGETABLES & FRUITS

92   Baked Sweet Potatoes

93   Blackberry Cobbler

94   Fire-and-Ice Kebabs

95   Fresh Vegetable Kebabs

96   Great Grilled Tofu

97   Grilled Apples

98   Grilled Caponata

99   Grilled Fruit Sundaes

100 Grilled Green Onions

101 Grilled Peaches

102 Grilled Pepper Sunburst

103 Grilled Pineapple with Brown Sugar Sauce

104 Grilled Polenta or Grits

105 Grilled Vidalia Onions

106 Herbed Vegetables on Skewers

107 Hot Potatoes

108 Maple Apple Rings

109 Marinated Tofu and Vegetable Brochettes

110 Michigan-Style Corn-on-the-Cob

111 New Potatoes on a Stick

112 Onion Lollipops

113 Super Grilled Salad

114 Zesty Italian Tomatoes

Baked Sweet Potatoes

Narcisse S. Cadgène
Free-Lance Writer, New York, NY

High in fiber, low in calories and full of nutrition, sweet potatoes aren't just for Thanksgiving. Their rich, slightly sweet flavor is a natural for the barbecue and, unlike corn or many other traditional grill foods, they're available all year — something for which my family certainly gives thanks! Like many of the best things in life, this recipe is simplicity itself.

Makes 4 servings

4 sweet potatoes, scrubbed   1 large lime, cut into 4 wedges
(about 1/2 pound each)

Prick sweet potatoes several times with a fork. If using a charcoal grill, place potatoes next to, but not on, the coals. If using a gas grill, wrap each potato in aluminum foil. Place potatoes on gas grill over medium heat. Cook, turning every 10 to 15 minutes, 45 to 60 minutes, or until fork-tender. In charcoal grill, sweet potato skins will turn black.

Cut a slit in each potato; fluff with a fork, and squeeze 1 lime wedge into each potato.

Blackberry Cobbler

Teri M. Grimes
Features Editor, *The Bradenton Herald*, Bradenton, FL

It's not often you think of cooking dessert on the grill, but it can be done. While the main course is cooking on the grill, heat the sweetened blackberries on top of the stove and mix up the dumpling batter. Once dinner is served, don't let those hot coals go to waste. Place the dessert right on the grill in a covered skillet. By the time dinner is over, dessert will be ready.

Makes 8 servings

4 cups blackberries
   (or blueberries)
1/2 cup plus 2 tablespoons
   granulated sugar, divided
2 tablespoons butter or margarine

1 cup buttermilk baking mix
1/3 cup light cream or
   half-and-half
Vanilla ice cream

In a 10-inch cast-iron skillet with a tight-fitting lid, combine blackberries and 1/2 cup sugar. Dot butter over berries. Cook over medium heat, stirring often, until bubbly. Keep hot.

In a medium mixing bowl, combine baking mix, remaining 2 tablespoons sugar and light cream; mix well. Spoon batter in eight mounds over hot berry mixture. Tightly cover skillet.

Place skillet on gas grill over medium-high heat or on charcoal grill 4 to 6 inches from medium-hot coals. Cover grill. Cook 15 to 20 minutes, or until dumplings are done.

Serve cobbler warm with scoops of vanilla ice cream.

Fire-and-Ice Kebabs

Zack Hanle
Editor at Large, *Bon Appétit*, New York, NY

Because my grilled fruit kebabs, which I often serve for dessert at outdoor feasts, became mushy and sloppy, I devised the idea of skewering the fruits ahead and freezing them. The fruits hold their shape, and the dessert can be prepared ahead of time. Hence the title for this delicious, healthful barbecue finale.

Makes 6 servings

1 can (17 ounces) apricot halves, unpeeled
1 can (8 ounces) pineapple chunks
1 can (11 ounces) mandarin orange segments
3 medium-size ripe bananas, peeled and cut into 1-inch chunks

1 package (7 ounces) flaked coconut
1/2 cup margarine or butter
1/2 cup firmly packed brown sugar

You will need six 12-inch skewers, either metal or bamboo. If using bamboo skewers, soak them in water 30 minutes to prevent burning.

Drain apricots, pineapple and mandarin oranges; discard juices or save for another use. Thread apricots, pineapple, mandarin oranges and banana alternately onto skewers. Pat skewered fruits dry with paper towels; roll skewers in coconut. Place skewers lengthwise across empty ice cube trays; let freeze solid (overnight).

When ready to serve, melt margarine in a small saucepan. Add brown sugar; mix well. Brush each frozen fruit kebab with brown sugar mixture.

Place kebabs on gas grill over medium heat or on charcoal grill 4 to 6 inches from medium coals. Cook, turning skewers as needed to prevent burning, about 10 minutes, or until golden brown.

Remember to Drive Smart and Drive Sober.

Fresh Vegetable Kebabs

Suzanne Hall
Food Editor, *The Chattanooga Times*, Chattanooga, TN

More than 47 percent of Tennessee's 26.3 million acres is farmland. Agriculture is the state's number one industry. Even when the weather doesn't cooperate fully (and most local farmers can't remember a recent year when it has), we still can find an abundant selection of fresh produce at reasonable prices. With the help of the county extension agent, I try to encourage readers to buy Tennessee produce by developing recipes such as this one.

Makes 4 servings

2 medium ears fresh corn	2 tablespoons finely chopped
2 medium zucchini	fresh chives
8 pearl onions	2 tablespoons finely chopped
1/2 cup butter or margarine,	fresh parsley
melted	1/2 teaspoon garlic salt

Remove husks and silk from corn. Slice corn and zucchini into 1-inch pieces. (An electric knife works well for cutting the corn.) Thread corn, zucchini and onions alternately on 4 metal skewers.

In a small bowl, combine butter, chives, parsley and garlic salt; mix well

Place kebabs on lightly oiled rack of gas grill over high heat or on charcoal grill about 3 inches from hot coals. Cook about 8 minutes, turning and brushing vegetables with butter sauce every 2 minutes.

Great Grilled Tofu

Lorrie Guttman
Food Editor, *Tallahassee Democrat*, Tallahassee, FL

While writing a feature about a couple who use tofu in everything from appetizers to desserts, I learned their secret for making tofu "meat-like." When tofu is frozen, it takes on a chewier texture. My family has had limited enthusiasm for tofu, so I decided to try freezing it, then marinating and grilling it. The tofu had a firm texture and delicious flavor, and my family liked it. I used a variation of a marinade originally meant for chicken.

Makes 4 servings

1 package (16 ounces) firm tofu, frozen
1/2 cup firmly packed brown sugar
1/2 cup reduced-sodium soy sauce
2 tablespoons fresh lime juice
6 cloves garlic, minced
1 teaspoon curry powder
1/4 teaspoon hot pepper sauce

Let frozen tofu thaw.

In a shallow dish, combine brown sugar, soy sauce, lime juice, garlic, curry powder and hot pepper sauce; mix well. Slice tofu about 1/2-inch thick; place slices in marinade and turn to coat each piece. Refrigerate, covered, 30 minutes; turn tofu slices and let marinate another 30 minutes.

Remove tofu slices from marinade; discard marinade. Place tofu on gas grill over medium heat or on charcoal grill 4 to 6 inches from medium coals. Cook about 10 minutes, or until tofu is lightly browned on both sides; turn once, using a wide spatula.

Grilled tofu goes well with rice, a green salad and fresh fruit.

Grilled Apples

Jane Gray
Food Editor, *Ludington Daily News*, Ludington, MI

You might not usually think of fruit as something to cook on the grill, but this easy recipe might change your mind. It combines the "over-the-coals" flavor that comes from grilling with the sweet juiciness of ripe apples. It's sure to please even the fussiest eater. Children love to help prepare this dish.

Makes 6 servings

6 large baking apples	1 cup chopped walnuts
1/2 cup orange marmalade	2 tablespoons lemon juice

Cut six squares (10 by 10 inches) of heavy-duty aluminum foil.

Core apples; remove peel from the upper part. Place one apple on each square of foil. Fill the center of each apple with orange marmalade; top with chopped walnuts. Sprinkle with lemon juice to keep cut surface from discoloring. Wrap foil around apple; twist the top to close. Refrigerate until ready to cook.

Place packets on gas grill over medium heat or on charcoal grill 6 to 8 inches from medium-hot coals. Cook 35 to 45 minutes, turning occasionally. Test for doneness by piercing with a fork through the foil. To serve, turn back the foil attractively to form a foil dish.

Grilled Caponata

Laura Barton
Free-Lance Writer, Portland, OR

My husband claims he dislikes eggplant, and usually grumbles when he sees me buying some at the store. But when I serve this dish that uses grilled eggplant and onions to make a flavorful Italian appetizer, he not only stops grumbling, he has seconds.

Makes about 1 quart

1 can (16 ounces) Italian plum tomatoes

2 tablespoons raisins

1/4 cup plus 2 tablespoons olive oil, divided

2 medium eggplants (about 8 1/2 inches long), cut into 1/2-inch slices

1 large red onion, cut into 1/2-inch slices

2 teaspoons unsweetened cocoa powder

20 capers

10 green olives, pitted and sliced

8 Kalamata olives, pitted and quartered (or pitted black olives)

3 tablespoons chopped fresh parsley

1/4 cup balsamic vinegar

Salt and black pepper, to taste

Drain tomatoes, reserving liquid; coarsely chop tomatoes and set aside. In a small saucepan, heat reserved tomato liquid to boiling. Remove from heat; add raisins. Let raisins soak 30 minutes.

Using about 2 tablespoons olive oil, lightly brush eggplant and onion slices on both sides with oil. Place vegetables on gas grill over medium-high heat or on charcoal grill 4 to 6 inches from medium-hot coals. Cook eggplant about 5 minutes per side, or until soft. Cook onion about 8 minutes per side, or until slightly charred and cooked through. Remove vegetables from grill; let cool.

In a large mixing bowl, combine reserved chopped tomatoes and cocoa powder; mix until cocoa dissolves. Drain raisins, discarding liquid. Add raisins, capers, green olives, Kalamata olives and parsley to tomato mixture; mix well.

Report suspected drunk drivers. You might be saving someone's life.

Coarsely chop grilled eggplant and onion; fold into tomato mixture. Add vinegar and remaining 1/4 cup olive oil. Season with salt and pepper. Let stand 30 minutes before serving. Serve at room temperature as an appetizer with French bread and crackers.

Note: Caponata can be prepared up to a week ahead and refrigerated.

Grilled Fruit Sundaes

Toni Burks
Free-Lance Writer, Roanoke, VA

If you've ever roasted marshmallows, you know the wonderful taste of something sweet cooked outdoors. This dessert is a fine celebration of a summer evening.

Makes 4 servings

1 large firm banana, peeled and cut into 1 1/2-inch chunks

4 slices (1/2-inch thick) fresh pineapple, peeled

4 scoops vanilla ice cream

Caramel sauce, warmed (see note)

1/4 cup toasted flaked coconut

If bamboo skewers are used, soak them in water 30 minutes to prevent burning. Thread banana chunks on bamboo or metal skewers.

Place pineapple slices and skewered bananas on oiled rack of gas grill over medium-high heat or on charcoal grill 4 to 6 inches from medium-hot coals. Cook 4 to 6 minutes, or until thoroughly heated, turning once.

Divide pineapple slices and banana pieces among 4 dessert dishes. Top each with a scoop of ice cream. Drizzle with warm caramel sauce; sprinkle with toasted coconut.

Note: The caramel apple dip available in the produce section of most supermarkets works well in this recipe.

Grilled Green Onions

Louise Dodd
Food Editor, *Courier Herald*, Dublin, GA

Nothing, except maybe a baked potato, exceeds green onions as an accompaniment to a good, thick, juicy steak. Your family or guests will be pleased with this flavor combination. Be sure to buy the largest green onions you can find, and while you're at it, you'd better get a large quantity, too.

Makes 8 to 12 servings

36 large green onions
1 cup olive oil
2 to 3 cloves garlic, minced

½ teaspoon freshly ground
black pepper
Salt, to taste

Trim onions, leaving about 2 inches of green top.

In a shallow dish, combine olive oil, garlic, pepper and salt. Add onions; stir to coat onions evenly. Refrigerate, covered, 1 hour, or overnight.

Drain onions; discard marinade. Place onions on gas grill over high heat or on charcoal grill 4 to 6 inches from hot coals. Cook, turning often, 4 to 5 minutes, or until lightly browned on all sides. Serve at room temperature. These hold nicely while you grill the steaks or other meat, if you can keep your guests from eating them.

Note: If using small green onions, you might want to bundle them together in small bunches so they do not slip through the grill, or cook them on a piece of heavy-duty aluminum foil.

Remind all passengers in your car to buckle up.

Grilled Peaches

Clara H. Eschmann
Food Columnist, *The Macon Telegraph*, Macon, GA

My father was a peach farmer, so naturally our family enjoyed this delicious fruit prepared in a variety of ways. My mother used to bake peaches in the oven, but modern cooks grill them. They are especially good as a side dish with poultry, ham or fresh pork, or they can be served as an easy dessert.

Makes 8 servings

8 firm peaches	1 cup granulated sugar, or less,
48 whole cloves	depending on sweetness
1 teaspoon ground cinnamon	of peaches

Rinse and peel peaches. Stick 6 whole cloves into each peach. In a small bowl, combine cinnamon and sugar; roll peaches in sugar-cinnamon mixture. Place each peach, stem-side down, on a square of heavy-duty aluminum foil. Sprinkle remaining sugar-cinnamon mixture over peaches; tightly close foil around each peach.

Place packets on gas grill over low heat or on charcoal grill 5 to 6 inches from low coals. (We often place these around the edges of the grill while cooking a slice of ham or other meat.) Cook 10 minutes, or until heated through.

Remove packets from grill. Carefully open packets and remove and discard cloves. The peaches are so juicy, it's a good idea to open each packet in a serving bowl in order to capture all the juice. Serve hot or cold as a side dish, or with ice cream, if desired, for dessert.

Note: Grilled peaches freeze well or can be refrigerated for use within a week.

Grilled Pepper Sunburst

Teri M. Grimes
Features Editor, *The Bradenton Herald*, Bradenton, FL

If Peter Piper were picking peppers today, he'd be in a pickle. Twenty years ago, the choice was easy: either green or red bell peppers. But now even the most mundane supermarket offers green, red, orange, yellow and even purple and black bell peppers. Although raw bell peppers taste pretty good, nothing beats the taste of a roasted pepper. This delightful recipe can cook right alongside chicken breasts or whatever you're having. The presentation is simply stunning and the taste is unbelievably good.

Makes 4 servings

2 pounds bell peppers
   (green, red, orange
   and yellow)
3 cloves garlic
1 teaspoon salt
1/4 cup olive oil
4 tablespoons balsamic vinegar,
   divided
1/2 teaspoon freshly ground
   black pepper
2 teaspoons finely chopped
   fresh oregano
   (or 1/2 teaspoon dried)

1 teaspoon finely chopped
   fresh rosemary
   (or 1/4 teaspoon dried)
1 teaspoon finely chopped fresh
   thyme (or 1/4 teaspoon dried)
1/4 pound feta cheese, drained
   and cut into 1/2-inch cubes
12 to 16 Kalamata olives
   (or any oil-cured olives)
French bread

Rinse peppers, then core and seed. Cut each pepper into thirds. Put pepper chunks in a large bowl.

Mash garlic and salt to a paste in a mortar with a pestle or the point of a sharp knife. In a small bowl, combine garlic-salt paste, olive oil, 3 tablespoons vinegar and pepper; mix well. Pour sauce over pepper chunks; toss to coat well.

When coals are hot, brush grill rack with a bit of oil to prevent sticking. Remove peppers from sauce, reserving sauce.

One out of every 200 babies born today will die in a crash with an intoxicated driver.

Place peppers, smooth-side down, on gas grill over high heat or on a charcoal grill 4 to 6 inches from hot coals. Cook 6 to 8 minutes, or until lightly charred but not mushy; baste with sauce and turn every 3 minutes. (Be sure to baste carefully so that the sauce does not drip onto the coals and cause a flare-up.)

Remove peppers from grill; slice into 1/2-inch-wide strips. Arrange strips on a platter in a sunburst pattern, alternating colors. Sprinkle with oregano, rosemary, thyme, feta cheese and olives. Drizzle remaining 1 tablespoon vinegar over peppers, if desired. Serve with lots of crusty French bread.

Note: If using dried herbs, soak them in the remaining 1 tablespoon balsamic vinegar for 5 minutes; sprinkle over peppers as directed.

Grilled Pineapple with Brown Sugar Sauce

Barbara Yost
Feature Writer, *The Phoenix Gazette*, Phoenix, AZ

> *This simple dessert tastes elegant and is the perfect finale to a hearty barbecue. You might want to cut the pineapple into chunks and serve it with the sauce over vanilla ice cream, pound cake or angel food cake.*

Makes 4 servings

6 tablespoons butter or margarine	2 teaspoons orange extract
1 cup firmly packed brown sugar	1 ripe pineapple
2 teaspoons vanilla	Grated orange peel, for garnish

In a saucepan over low heat, melt butter. Add brown sugar; stir constantly until sugar is almost dissolved. Texture may remain slightly grainy. Remove from heat. Add vanilla and orange extract; mix well. Set aside but do not refrigerate.

Trim, core and peel pineapple. Cut into four 1 1/2-inch thick rounds.

Oil the grill rack or spray it with nonstick cooking spray. Place pineapple rounds on gas grill over medium heat or on charcoal grill 4 to 6 inches from medium coals. Cook 3 to 4 minutes per side. Remove from heat; top with brown sugar sauce. Garnish each serving with orange peel.

Grilled Polenta or Grits

Narcisse S. Cadgène
Free-Lance Writer, New York, NY

Traditionally made slowly and painstakingly on top of the stove, polenta is often then sautéed in a pan. I throw tradition out the window, literally, and my polenta winds up on the grill. Polenta is a wonderful accompaniment to almost any barbecue, from chicken to fish, but the corn and garlic flavor go especially well with either traditional barbecue sauces (where I might otherwise serve corn bread on the side) or anything seasoned with basil, such as a pesto.

Makes 4 to 6 servings

4 cups water, divided
1 cup yellow cornmeal (or grits)
1/2 teaspoon salt
1 clove garlic, pressed
2 tablespoons grated Parmesan or Romano cheese

Vegetable oil
Grated Parmesan or Romano cheese, for garnish

Pour about 1 cup water into a large (at least 2 quarts) microwave-safe bowl. Gradually stir in the cornmeal, adding water as necessary, to make a smooth paste. Stir in remaining water and salt. Microwave, uncovered, on High (100%) power 5 minutes. Stir mixture, eliminating any lumps. Add garlic; mix well. Microwave, covered, on High 6 minutes. Stir in 2 tablespoons grated cheese.

(To cook on stovetop, put all of the water in a saucepan; bring to a boil. Reduce heat; stir in cornmeal, salt and garlic. Cook, stirring frequently, 10 to 15 minutes, or until mixture thickens. Stir in cheese.)

Pour polenta into a lightly oiled 9x9x2-inch pan. Refrigerate until well chilled and set.

Cut polenta into 3-inch squares or any shape that is large enough to balance on a grill rack. Lightly brush polenta with oil. Place polenta on gas grill over medium heat or on charcoal grill 4 to 6 inches from medium coals. Cook 4 to 5 minutes per side, or until heated through and lightly browned. Serve hot, dusted with additional grated cheese, if desired.

Grilled Vidalia Onions

Clara H. Eschmann
Food Columnist, *The Macon Telegraph*, Macon, GA

Georgians are proud of the state's sweet Vidalia onions, which now are widely available in markets across the country. This recipe also can be used with sweet onions of your choice. The Georgia ones are an early spring crop and can be stored into the fall. A reader sent me this recipe, to which I added parsley.

Makes 6 servings

6 large Vidalia or sweet onions
6 tablespoons butter or
   margarine, melted

6 chicken or beef bouillon cubes
6 teaspoons finely chopped fresh
   parsley (or 3 teaspoons dried)

Peel onions; wipe with a damp cloth. Rub lightly with some of the melted butter. With a sharp pointed knife, cut a hole 2 inches in diameter and 1 inch deep in the top of each onion. Place 1 bouillon cube and 1 teaspoon fresh parsley (1/2 teaspoon dried) in hole in each onion; top each with an equal portion of remaining butter.

Place each onion, top-side up, on a square of heavy-duty aluminum foil; seal foil around each onion.

Place packets on gas grill over medium heat or on charcoal grill 4 to 5 inches from medium coals. Cook 20 to 30 minutes, or until fork-tender.

There will be a large amount of juice in the foil, so it is a good idea to open the packets over a plate or bowl in order to capture the juices, which can then be poured over onion or meat. The juices are too good to lose!

Note: The foil-wrapped grilled onions can be frozen and reheated.

Herbed Vegetables on Skewers

Jeanne Voltz
Cookbook Author, Pittsboro, NC

With careful cutting and threading onto skewers, any vegetable can be cooked on the grill. Leave the peel on for stability, then pull it off after cooking. Smoky flavor does wonders for eggplant and soft squash. Season the veggies well, and taste the difference that grilling makes.

Makes about 4 servings

1 tablespoon red wine vinegar
1 tablespoon water or
    chicken broth
1 teaspoon granulated sugar
1/2 teaspoon salt
1/4 teaspoon freshly ground
    black pepper
1/4 cup olive oil
1 to 2 cloves garlic, minced
8 to 12 fresh mushrooms

1 large eggplant, cut into
    thick cubes
2 yellow squash, cut into chunks
1 to 2 bell peppers (any color),
    seeded and cut into
    large squares
2 medium onions, cut into wedges
2 teaspoons dried rosemary,
    thyme or marjoram

In a small bowl, combine vinegar, water, sugar, salt and pepper. Stir to dissolve sugar and salt. Stir in olive oil and garlic; mix well. Pour mixture into a resealable plastic bag or deep bowl.

Rinse mushrooms. Put mushrooms in a small saucepan and cover with lightly salted water. Boil 2 minutes; drain well. (Precooking the mushrooms prevents them from splitting on the grill.)

Add mushrooms, eggplant, squash, bell peppers and onions to oil mixture; toss to coat vegetables with oil mixture. Refrigerate, covered, at least 1 hour.

Drain vegetables, reserving marinade. Thread vegetables on metal skewers, mixing or matching as you choose. Some vegetables are less susceptible to tearing if speared diagonally. Squash sections are best threaded through a part with peel on it. Mushrooms work best if speared through the caps and stems. Sprinkle skewered vegetables with some of the rosemary.

Alcohol involvement is highest in single-vehicle crashes between 9 p.m. - 6 a.m.

Place skewers on gas grill over high heat or on charcoal grill 4 to 6 inches from hot coals. Cook 10 to 20 minutes, turning to cook evenly; brush frequently with reserved marinade and sprinkle with remaining rosemary. Serve hot with grilled meats.

Hot Potatoes

Beth Whitley Duke
Food Editor, *Amarillo Globe-News*, Amarillo, TX

Baked potatoes are the usual accompaniment to grilled steaks. After all, nothing is easier than washing potatoes, wrapping them in foil and putting them on the grill or in the oven. The problem with baked potatoes is that you have to serve an assortment of condiments to meet contemporary tastes: butter, sour cream, chives, bacon, etc. This recipe puts the condiments inside and lets the flavors bake with the potato. The results are a happy surprise for guests who peel back the foil and find that someone has already dressed their potatoes. The cook gets a break, too, with simplified serving and clean-up.

Makes 8 servings

8 large baking potatoes, scrubbed
2 large onions, sliced thin
1/2 cup butter or margarine
2 tablespoons seasoned salt
1 teaspoon garlic powder
1/2 cup sliced fresh mushrooms
1/2 cup grated Parmesan cheese

Place each potato on a square of heavy-duty aluminum foil large enough to generously wrap the potato. Slit potato crosswise at 1/4-inch intervals, being careful not to cut all the way through. Fill slits by putting an onion slice in one and a pat of butter in the next, and repeating.

In a small bowl, combine seasoned salt and garlic powder. Sprinkle over each potato. Top each potato with a generous spoonful of mushrooms. Bring the foil over the potato and wrap it; seal the edges carefully.

Place potatoes on gas grill over high heat or on charcoal grill 4 inches from hot coals. Cook 1 hour, or until potatoes are done. Serve in foil packets. Pass Parmesan cheese to sprinkle over each potato.

Maple Apple Rings

Sally Scherer
Food Writer, *The Macon Telegraph*, Macon, GA

I made this recipe for the first time at a Girl Scout cookout when I was a young girl living in Illinois. I don't use the recipe often, but when I do I'm always reminded of those childhood days. Over the years, I've varied the recipe by changing the spices and nuts and adding raisins.

Makes 4 servings

4 medium baking apples, cored
    and thinly sliced into rings
8 teaspoons maple-flavored syrup
2 teaspoons margarine or
    butter, melted

1/2 teaspoon ground cinnamon
1/8 teaspoon ground nutmeg
1/4 cup chopped walnuts
1/4 cup raisins

Arrange an equal amount of apple rings on each of 4 large squares of heavy-duty aluminum foil.

In a small mixing bowl, combine syrup, margarine, cinnamon, nutmeg, walnuts and raisins; mix well. Spoon an equal amount of syrup mixture over each set of apple rings. Wrap securely, sealing edges of foil well.

Place packets on gas grill over medium heat or on charcoal grill 4 to 6 inches from medium coals. Cook 15 minutes, or until apples are tender. Serve hot.

6 ounces of pure alcohol is equal to about 12 bottles of beer or 8 mixed drinks.

Marinated Tofu and Vegetable Brochettes

Laura Barton
Free-lance Writer, Portland, OR

Several years ago, before it was fashionable to eat vegetarian, I tentatively served a side dish of skewered marinated tofu cubes at a barbecue party. To my surprise, the dish was the hit of the party and disappeared before the meat dishes. I am no longer tentative about serving grilled tofu. The trick to grilling tofu successfully is to use firm tofu. Weighing down the tofu and draining excess moisture will help the tofu stay together on the grill.

Makes 20 servings

1 package (16 ounces) firm tofu, well drained
3 tablespoons vegetable oil
3 tablespoons soy sauce
2 teaspoons ground ginger
1 teaspoon sesame oil
1 teaspoon onion powder
1/2 teaspoon garlic powder

3 bell peppers, cut into chunks (use a combination of green, red and yellow bell peppers for color contrast)
2 zucchini, cut into 1/2-inch pieces
50 small to medium button mushrooms

Slice tofu horizontally into two layers, then cut each layer into 25 pieces; drain well.

In a shallow dish, combine vegetable oil, soy sauce, ginger, sesame oil, onion powder and garlic powder; mix well. Add tofu cubes; spoon marinade over tofu to coat. Refrigerate, covered, 2 to 3 hours, turning tofu occasionally to coat well.

Remove tofu from marinade; reserve marinade. Put marinade in saucepan and heat to boiling. Reduce heat and let marinade simmer until needed.

Thread tofu cubes, bell pepper chunks, zucchini pieces and mushrooms alternately on metal, bamboo or wooden skewers. (Bamboo or wooden skewers should be soaked in water 30 minutes to prevent burning.) Place skewers on gas grill over medium heat or on charcoal grill 4 to 6 inches from medium coals. Cook about 10 minutes, or until vegetables are tender, basting with heated marinade. Discard remaining marinade.

Experts say that direct costs of drunk driving in the U.S total $44 billion each year.

Michigan-Style Corn-on-the-Cob

Ann Corell Wells
Food Editor, *The Grand Rapids Press*, Grand Rapids, MI

For many years, my family celebrated Labor Day with a corn grill at our cottage on Lake Michigan. My brother was always in charge of grilling the corn and this is his technique. For Labor Day gatherings, several bushels of fresh-picked corn were consumed. Diners husk their own ears, so you'll want to provide extra pot holders or mitts. An easy way to butter the corn is to pour melted butter into glass jars or pitchers and let guests dip the corn into the butter. Provide lots of paper napkins. This is messy, but wonderful, eating. This recipe has been pared down for smaller groups, but you'll want to plan on at least two ears of corn for each person. This corn is so good you'll never cook it any other way in the summer.

Makes 8 servings

16 ears fresh corn, unhusked
2 gallons cold water
Melted butter

Salt, black pepper, Parmesan cheese or other seasonings, to taste (optional)

Put corn in a large container; pour cold water over the corn. Soak at least 30 minutes. Drain.

Place unhusked ears of corn on gas grill over high heat or on charcoal grill about 4 inches from hot coals. With tongs, turn ears to prevent the husks from burning. Cook 15 to 20 minutes.

Let each diner peel the husks. Husks and silk do not have to be completely removed; the husks make good handles. Corn will be very hot, so use hot pads, mitts or kitchen towels to remove husks.

Pour melted butter into jars or pitchers and dip corn into the butter. Season to taste, if desired, but the corn is so good it needs no seasoning.

Drunk driving is the most frequently committed violent crime in America.

New Potatoes on a Stick

Paula M. Galusha
Free-Lance Home Economist, Tulsa, OK

Small potatoes can be cooked on a covered grill in about the same time a steak cooks. A large lid can be used if you don't have a covered grill. New potatoes are always such a welcome sight, but new potatoes with parsley can get boring, so we often prepare ours this way. The recipe was inspired by a similar dish in a restaurant years ago.

Makes 4 to 6 servings

12 small new potatoes
   (about 2 ounces each)
Vegetable oil
1/2 cup olive oil
6 tablespoons cider vinegar
1 teaspoon Dijon-style mustard

1/2 teaspoon salt
Dash hot pepper sauce
1/4 cup finely chopped
   green onions
2 tablespoons chopped fresh
   basil (or 1 tablespoon dried)

Rinse potatoes; pat dry with paper towels. Lightly coat with vegetable oil. Thread 3 or 4 potatoes on each metal skewer, leaving space between potatoes.

Place skewers on gas grill over medium heat or on charcoal grill 4 to 6 inches from medium coals. Cook 20 to 25 minutes, turning once, or until tender.

Meanwhile, combine olive oil, vinegar, mustard, salt and hot pepper sauce; mix well.

When potatoes are tender, remove from skewers and place on a platter with a rim. Cut an "X" in top of each potato and squeeze just until it opens slightly. Sprinkle potatoes with green onions and basil; pour dressing over potatoes. Turn to coat potatoes. Serve at once.

Onion Lollipops

Narcisse S. Cadgène
Free-Lance Writer, New York, NY

Grilled vegetables are wonderful, and onions are a special favorite. However, I've fished out many a lost veggie that succumbed to gravity and slipped through the grill rack. These neat, easy onion slices solve that problem because they come not only with support, but also with a handle.

Makes 6 servings

1 extra-large Spanish onion, 4 inches or more in diameter	1 tablespoon vegetable oil or olive oil
1 tablespoon balsamic or red wine vinegar	Freshly ground black pepper, to taste
1 teaspoon granulated sugar	

Soak 6 to 8 bamboo skewers in water 30 minutes before using, so they will not burn on the grill.

Peel onion; pull off any long trailing roots, but do not cut off the root itself. Place the onion on its side (root to the left and stem end to the right). Hold onion firmly with one hand. Beginning about 1/2 inch from the stem end, carefully push a skewer through onion, as straight up-and-down as possible. With a sharp knife, take a vertical slice off the uneven stem end about 1/4 inch to the right of the skewer; discard this small piece. Next, cut vertically through the onion about 1/4 inch to the left of the skewer. What results is a 1/2-inch onion slice on a skewer. Carefully push the skewer through the last layer of onion.

Repeat for the next slice, using another skewer. Skewer and slice the entire onion, except the last thin slice containing the root, which should be discarded.

Sprinkle slices with vinegar, then with sugar. Let stand a few minutes so vinegar penetrates and sugar dissolves, or refrigerate until ready to grill. Before grilling, brush slices with oil. Place onion slices on gas grill over medium heat or on charcoal grill 4 to 6 inches from medium-hot coals. Cook about 5 minutes per side. The "lollipops" should be soft but not mushy, and nicely browned.

Before serving, give each slice one twist of the pepper grinder.

About 21 billion miles were driven drunk.

Super Grilled Salad

Jim Hillibish
City Editor, *The Repository*, Canton, OH

Perhaps this recipe began when somebody dropped a salad bowl onto a lighted grill. Anyway, it makes for excellent and unusual eating, and your guests will be taken aback. The vegetable flavors meld, accentuated by the charcoal smoke. Appoint someone to keep an eye on it during grilling because overcooking is an ever-present danger.

Makes 3 servings

1 medium head radicchio or 6 Belgian endives	3 medium tomatoes, quartered
12 small sweet onions	2 tablespoons olive oil
	1 tablespoon dried basil

Cut radicchio into thirds or endives into halves lengthwise; cut through the heart to keep sections from separating.

Place onions in a saucepan; add water to cover. Boil 5 minutes. Drain well.

Put radicchio, onions and tomatoes on a large square of heavy-duty aluminum foil. Sprinkle with olive oil and basil. Close foil securely around vegetables.

Place packet on gas grill over medium heat or on charcoal grill 4 to 6 inches from medium coals. Punch 6 to 8 holes in foil to allow smoke to rise through the vegetables. Cook, turning often, 15 to 20 minutes, or until vegetables are hot. Serve hot.

Zesty Italian Tomatoes

Sally Scherer
Food Writer, *The Macon Telegraph*, Macon, GA

There's nothing better than home-grown Georgia tomatoes. We eat them in various ways throughout their peak growing time. This recipe was created by a friend who wanted an easy side dish to go with grilled meats. These tomatoes are simple and so good.

Makes 2 servings

1 large tomato
1 tablespoon bottled Italian
   salad dressing
1/2 teaspoon dried basil

Salt and black pepper, to taste
1 1/2 teaspoons butter or
   margarine, melted
1/3 cup dry bread crumbs

Cut tomato in half crosswise. Sprinkle each half with equal amounts of Italian dressing, basil, salt and pepper. Combine butter and bread crumbs; spoon over tomato halves.

Place tomato halves, topping-side up, on a piece of heavy-duty aluminum foil. Seal foil, leaving a small opening for steam to escape. Place foil packet on gas grill over high heat or on charcoal grill 4 to 6 inches from hot coals. Cook 10 minutes, or until done. Serve hot.

A .02 BAC can affect driving abilities and increase the chances of a crash.

Sauces & Marinades

116   Apple-Tarragon Marinade

117   Buttermilk Marinades

118   Cincinnati Dry Rub

119   Chuckwagon Rub

120   Compound Butters

121   Cucumber Sauce

122   Curried Fruit Glaze

123   Dad's Smoking Sauce

124   Fish Coating

125   Fresh Tuna Marinade

126   Herb-Garlic Rub

127   Healthful Marinade

127   Honey-Mustard Glaze

128   Jamaican-Style Jerk Rub

129   Mom's Barbecue Sauce

129   Multi-Purpose Marinade

130   Mustard Steak Rub

131   Oriental Lemon Marinade

132   Peach Salsa

133   Shish Kebab Marinade

134   Strawberry-Mustard Brush

Apple-Tarragon Marinade

Debra Carr-Elsing
Food Writer, *The Capital Times*, Madison, WI

This is the kind of recipe that makes people ask, "What's in it?" The sweet flavor of honey balances the strong onion flavor. It's a combination that works, especially when the distinctive flavor of tarragon is added. Beef is a possibility here, but this marinade is outstanding on chicken or lamb. This recipe makes enough marinade for about four pounds of chicken, lamb or beef.

Makes about 2¹/₂ cups

1 cup apple cider
¹/₂ cup cider vinegar
¹/₂ cup vegetable oil
¹/₃ cup sliced green onions
3 tablespoons honey
2 tablespoons steak sauce

2 teaspoons chopped
   fresh tarragon
1 teaspoon salt
¹/₄ teaspoon freshly ground
   black pepper

In medium saucepan, combine cider, vinegar, oil, green onions, honey, steak sauce, tarragon, salt and pepper; mix well. Bring to a boil; reduce heat and simmer, uncovered, 20 minutes. Let cool. Refrigerate, covered, until needed.

Use as a marinade for chicken, lamb, or beef. Discard marinade after use.

The risk of a crash increases greatly at a .05 blood alcohol content.

Buttermilk Marinades

Laura Barton
Free-Lance Writer, Portland, OR

I enjoy developing great-tasting marinades and sauces that are flavorful and seal in moisture, yet are not high in fat. Buttermilk provides a tangy base for a variety of marinade seasonings. Each of these variations makes enough to marinate one pound (about four servings) of meat, such as pork tenderloin, turkey cutlets or boned, skinned chicken breasts.

Makes about 2 cups each

For Zesty Italian Buttermilk Marinade:

2 cups buttermilk
3 cloves garlic, minced
1 tablespoon red wine vinegar
1 tablespoon grated
    Parmesan cheese
2 teaspoons dried oregano
2 teaspoons dried rosemary

2 teaspoons dried basil
    (or 2 tablespoons
    finely chopped fresh)
1 teaspoon dried thyme
1 teaspoon finely chopped
    fresh parsley

For Southwest-Style Buttermilk Marinade:

2 cups buttermilk
1/4 cup finely chopped fresh
    cilantro (optional)
3 cloves garlic, minced
2 tablespoons onion powder

1 tablespoon chili powder
2 teaspoons ground cumin
1 teaspoon dried oregano
1 teaspoon Worcestershire sauce
1/2 teaspoon hot pepper sauce

For Zesty Italian Buttermilk Marinade: Combine buttermilk, garlic, vinegar, cheese, oregano, rosemary, basil, thyme and parsley in a medium mixing bowl; mix well.

For Southwest-Style Buttermilk Marinade: Combine buttermilk, cilantro, garlic, onion powder, chili powder, cumin, oregano, Worcestershire sauce and hot pepper sauce in a medium mixing bowl; mix well.

Refrigerate Buttermilk Marinade, covered, until needed. Use as a marinade for pork, turkey, chicken or other meats. Discard marinade after use.

Cincinnati Dry Rub

Jim Hillibish
City Editor, *The Repository*, Canton, OH

Dry rubs began as a way to preserve meat. They've evolved into a quick way to flavor meat for the grill. They store well and are ready at the twist of a jar lid. Cincinnati Dry Rub possibly has its roots in the Ohio riverboat trade. Riverboats passed through many communities, adding regional food favorites to their galley menus. The result: This rub combines elements of Louisiana Cajun and Tennessee flatlands cookery. This recipe makes enough rub for 3 to 4 pounds of meat.

Makes about 3/4 cup

4 tablespoons black peppercorns

3 dried whole chili peppers
(or 2 tablespoons chili powder)

2 bay leaves

2 tablespoons dried oregano

2 tablespoons dried parsley

2 tablespoons dried grated
lemon or lime peel

1 tablespoon chopped dried
mushrooms

1 teaspoon ground cumin

1 teaspoon garlic powder

1 teaspoon dry mustard

In container of electric blender, combine peppercorns, dried chili peppers, bay leaves, oregano, parsley, lemon peel, dried mushrooms, cumin, garlic powder and dry mustard; grind to a coarse powder. Store in a tightly sealed container up to six months in the freezer.

To use: Coat beef or pork roasts evenly with rub. Refrigerate, covered, at least 5 hours, or overnight, before grilling. Discard excess rub that has been in contact with raw meat.

No one is safe from people who drive under the influence of alcohol.

Chuckwagon Rub

Beth Whitley Duke
Food Editor, *Amarillo Globe-News*, Amarillo, TX

Col. Charles Goodnight, a famous Texas pioneer, invented the chuckwagon to accommodate the long cattle drives across the Texas plains. The chuckwagon was a model of efficient engineering because it had to hold enough provisions for 25 or 30 cowboys on trail drives that lasted weeks. When the chuckwagon got close to a town, the cook would stock up on coffee, dried beans, cornmeal, flour, sugar and salt. The wagon also held bedrolls, lanterns, tarps, a keg of horseshoes and a barrel of water in case the cowboys had to make camp between watering holes. Cowboy recipes have their own flavor. They never tasted the same way twice. If the cook ran out of something, he would substitute something else, such as molasses for sugar. That is one reason why no two barbecue rub recipes in Texas are ever exactly alike. This barbecue rub is a contemporary adaptation of an old-time ranch recipe. We call it a rub because it works best when you use a clean dish mop to rub the sauce right into the meat. Use it on chicken, ribs, pork or the Texas favorite, beef.

Makes about 3 cups

2 tablespoons bacon drippings
  (or vegetable oil)
1 medium onion, chopped
1 clove garlic, minced
1 bottle (14 ounces) ketchup
1/2 cup Worcestershire sauce

1/4 cup brown sugar
1/4 cup water
1/2 teaspoon salt
1/2 teaspoon hot pepper sauce
1/2 teaspoon dry mustard

Heat bacon drippings in a medium saucepan. Add onion and garlic; cook until tender. Add ketchup, Worcestershire sauce, brown sugar, water, salt, hot pepper sauce and dry mustard; mix well. Bring to a boil. Reduce heat to low; simmer, stirring often, 15 minutes.

Remove from heat; let sauce cool. Refrigerate, covered, until needed.

To use: Pour sauce into saucepan; place saucepan on grill and let sauce heat alongside the meat. Brush or swab sauce onto meat during grilling; discard remaining sauce.

Compound Butters

Narcisse S. Cadgène
Free-Lance Writer, New York, NY

Compound butters are a quick and simple way to add flavor and moisture to grilled foods. They are particularly well suited to fish, chicken and vegetables, although a pat of compound butter on a steak is a classic French entrée. These three "starter" recipes should stimulate any innovative cook's imagination to produce original recipes. Each recipe makes about eight servings.

Makes about 2/3 cup each

For Oriental Garlic Butter for Vegetables:

1/2 cup unsalted butter, at room temperature
4 large cloves garlic, minced

2 tablespoons soy sauce
1 teaspoon grated fresh ginger
1 teaspoon granulated sugar

For Dill and Lemon Butter for Seafood:

1/2 cup salted or unsalted butter, at room temperature
1/4 cup chopped fresh dill

1/2 teaspoon lemon juice
1/4 teaspoon finely grated lemon peel

For Spicy Cajun Butter for Chicken, Fish or Meat:

1/2 cup unsalted butter, at room temperature
2 teaspoons salt
2 teaspoons paprika
1 1/2 teaspoons black pepper

1 1/2 teaspoons garlic powder
1 teaspoon onion powder
3/4 teaspoon cayenne pepper
2/3 teaspoon dried thyme
3/4 teaspoon dried oregano

For Oriental Garlic Butter: Combine butter, garlic, soy sauce, ginger and sugar in work bowl of food processor fitted with steel blade or in mixing bowl of electric mixer. Process or mix until smooth.

For Dill and Lemon Butter: Combine butter, dill, lemon juice and lemon peel in work bowl of food processor fitted with steel blade or in mixing bowl of electric mixer. Process or mix until smooth.

Drunk driving deaths have decreased more than 38% since MADD was founded.

For Spicy Cajun Butter: Combine butter, salt, paprika, pepper, garlic powder, onion powder, cayenne, thyme and oregano in work bowl of food processor fitted with steel blade or in mixing bowl of electric mixer. Process or mix until smooth.

To complete each Compound Butter: Roll butter mixture in plastic wrap, shaping mixture into a log about the diameter of a half-dollar. Twist ends of plastic wrap to close; refrigerate or freeze until needed. Slice off thin rounds of butter mixture; use to baste food as it grills. Just before serving, top each serving with a pat of butter mixture.

(Or, pack butter mixture in a small crock; refrigerate, covered, until firm. Serve directly from the crock at the table or use a melon baller to make individual servings.)

Store unused Compound Butter, covered, in the freezer for several weeks. Slice off or spoon out butter as needed.

Cucumber Sauce

Debra Carr-Elsing
Food Writer, *The Capital Times*, Madison, WI

I like to use my fresh garden produce for outdoor cookouts. This recipe calls for both cucumbers and green onions. I also like the fact that this recipe supports my state's many dairy farmers. With the tartness of grated lemon peel and the strong flavor of onions, this obviously isn't a sweet sauce. Watch out — it packs a mild punch. This makes enough sauce for about 3 pounds of chicken, fish or pork.

Makes about 1¹/₂ cups

1 cup peeled, finely chopped cucumber	1 tablespoon sliced green onion
¹/₃ cup sour cream	1 teaspoon grated lemon peel
¹/₃ cup mayonnaise	¹/₄ teaspoon dried dill weed

In medium mixing bowl, combine cucumber, sour cream, mayonnaise, green onion, lemon peel and dill weed; mix well. Refrigerate, covered, at least 1 hour.

Serve sauce with grilled chicken, fish or pork.

Curried Fruit Glaze

Gail Bellamy
Senior Editor, *Restaurant Hospitality*, Cleveland, OH

This recipe is a versatile, forgiving one. I've experimented with various versions — using Dijon-style mustard rather than dry mustard; adding minced garlic; adding freshly grated ginger; and using peach preserves rather than apricot spreadable fruit. The flavors of the glaze marry well with scallops or shrimp. The seafood should be lightly coated with the glaze (a pastry brush works well) and allowed to marinate before grilling.

Makes about 1/2 cup

3 tablespoons olive oil
1/4 cup plus 1 tablespoon apricot
   spreadable fruit
1 tablespoon raspberry vinegar
   or cider vinegar

1/4 teaspoon dry mustard
1 teaspoon curry powder

In small bowl, combine olive oil, spreadable fruit, vinegar, dry mustard and curry powder; mix well. Refrigerate, covered, until needed.

To use: Put 1 pound large shrimp or sea scallops in shallow dish; pour glaze over shrimp and turn to lightly coat each piece. Refrigerate, covered, 2 to 3 hours, or longer, before grilling. Discard glaze after use.

In 1993, the impaired driving death toll was approximately 17,461.

Dad's Smoking Sauce

Carolyn Flournoy
Food Columnist, *The Times*, Shreveport, LA

In the early days of our marriage, with four children to raise on two slim salaries, we had to devise Christmas gifts for friends that would not wreck the budget. We chose food (of course!) and gave gift sacks containing smoked chicken, rolls and a small jar of homemade mayonnaise. The secret of our success was Dad's Smoking Sauce (created by Mom), and our gifts became much coveted. Because everyone is watching fat and cholesterol, we now include a jar of commercial green peppercorn mustard instead of homemade mayonnaise. Last year, one of our sons gave us sacks imprinted, "Another smoked chicken."

Makes about 3½ cups

2 cups margarine	1 tablespoon cider vinegar
1 cup water	1 tablespoon dried parsley
¼ cup lemon juice	½ teaspoon liquid smoke
2 tablespoons Worcestershire sauce	½ teaspoon salt
2 tablespoons light soy sauce	¼ teaspoon garlic powder

In a large saucepan with a heavy bottom, combine margarine, water, lemon juice, Worcestershire sauce, soy sauce, vinegar, parsley, liquid smoke, salt and garlic powder; mix well. Bring to a boil. Reduce heat to low; simmer 30 minutes. Remove from heat; let sauce cool. Refrigerate, covered, until needed.

To use: Pour sauce into saucepan; place saucepan on grill and let sauce heat alongside the poultry. Brush or swab sauce onto chicken or turkey during grilling or smoking; discard remaining sauce.

Note: To speed the cooking process, generously coat chicken with sauce and roast in a preheated 450° oven 25 minutes. Coat chicken again with sauce and cook over hot coals in a covered grill 15 to 20 minutes, or until done. Leave skin on during grilling to help retain juices; remove skin before eating, if desired.

Fish Coating

Stacy Lam
Reporter, *The Macon Telegraph*, Macon, GA

Although I usually use some sort of marinade for grilled fish, I recently decided to try this coating, which I've used for baking and frying fish, to see how it worked on the grill. The results were great. The coating is especially good on trout and red snapper.

Makes about 1 1/2 cups

1 cup chopped or slivered almonds
1/2 cup grated Parmesan cheese
1/2 teaspoon garlic salt
1/2 teaspoon poultry seasoning
1/2 teaspoon paprika
1/2 teaspoon dried dill weed
1/4 teaspoon black pepper

Using a food processor or electric blender, process almonds until finely ground. Add Parmesan cheese, garlic salt, poultry seasoning, paprika, dill weed and pepper; mix well. Refrigerate, covered, until needed.

To use: Put coating in a shallow dish or spread it on a large piece of waxed paper. Dip fish pieces in lemon juice, then roll in coating until well covered. Grill as desired. Discard remaining coating.

About 48 people are killed each day in alcohol-related crashes.

Fresh Tuna Marinade

Beth W. Orenstein
Free-Lance Writer, Northampton, PA

I like grilled fresh tuna because of its full flavor and firm texture. This is one of my favorite marinades for tuna; it also goes well with salmon steaks. This recipe makes enough marinade for about two tuna steaks.

Makes about 1 cup

¹/₂ cup soy sauce
¹/₂ cup rice vinegar
2 cloves garlic, minced
2 tablespoons honey

2 teaspoons toasted sesame seeds
1 teaspoon ground ginger
¹/₂ teaspoon lemon-pepper
   seasoning

In a small bowl, combine soy sauce, vinegar, garlic, honey, sesame seeds, ginger and lemon pepper; mix well. Refrigerate, covered, until needed.

To use: Pour marinade over tuna in a shallow dish. Refrigerate, covered, at least 1 hour. Remove tuna from marinade; discard marinade. Grill tuna as desired.

Herb-Garlic Rub

Jane Gray
Food Editor, *Ludington Daily News*, Ludington, MI

This all-purpose recipe is a timesaver when you aren't sure what type of meat, poultry or fish you plan to grill — it goes with almost everything. It can be prepared ahead of time and refrigerated until you're ready to use it. You can vary the herbs to suit individual tastes. You might want to mix up an extra batch to sprinkle over steamed summer vegetables.

Makes about 1/2 cup

2 tablespoons minced fresh parsley
2 tablespoons minced fresh
 oregano (or 2 teaspoons dried)
1 1/2 teaspoons minced fresh
 rosemary (or 1/2 teaspoon dried)
1 1/2 teaspoons minced fresh thyme
 (or 1/2 teaspoon dried)

1 tablespoon minced fresh garlic
1 1/2 teaspoons salt, or to taste
1 1/2 teaspoons freshly ground
 black pepper, or to taste
1 teaspoon cayenne pepper,
 or to taste

In a small bowl, combine parsley, oregano, rosemary, thyme, garlic, salt, pepper and cayenne; mix well. Refrigerate, covered, until needed.

To use: Rub herb mixture over surface of meat, poultry or fish. Let stand at room temperature 30 minutes, then grill as desired. Discard excess rub that has come in contact with raw meat, poultry or fish.

About 950,000 persons were injured in alcohol-related crashes in 1993.

Healthful Marinade

Gail Bellamy
Senior Editor, *Restaurant Hospitality*, Cleveland, OH

Marinating adds more flavor than basting does to grilled fish. This quick and easy no-oil marinade requires no exotic ingredients and practically no preparation time. Higher-fat fish (such as salmon, mackerel, trout or mahi-mahi) stand up well to the rigors of grilling, but they still benefit from a flavorful marinade. This recipe makes enough to marinate about one pound of fish steaks or fillets.

Makes 1 cup

¹/₂ cup pineapple juice   ¹/₂ cup teriyaki sauce

In a shallow dish, combine pineapple juice and teriyaki sauce; mix well.

To use: Add fish steaks or fillets to marinade. Refrigerate, covered, 1 to 2 hours. Remove fish from marinade; discard marinade. Grill fish as desired.

Honey-Mustard Glaze

Jane Gray
Food Editor, *Ludington Daily News*, Ludington, MI

The simplicity of this glaze for pork or poultry is one of the reasons it's a favorite among chefs I know. The glaze can be prepared ahead of time and refrigerated, with only a quick stir needed before using.

Makes about ¹/₂ cup

5 tablespoons honey   2 tablespoons brown sugar
2 tablespoons coarse-grain
    Dijon-style mustard

In a small saucepan, combine honey, mustard and brown sugar; mix well. Simmer over low heat 5 minutes, or until sugar melts. Remove from heat and let cool. Refrigerate, covered, until needed.

To use: Stir to mix ingredients. Brush glaze on poultry or pork during the last 5 to 10 minutes of grilling. Discard remaining glaze.

Jamaican-Style Jerk Rub

Barbara Gibbs Ostmann
Food Writer, St. Louis, MO

We first sampled jerk pork on a Jamaican vacation about 10 years ago. Since then, Caribbean restaurants have popped up in major cities around the United States and jerk has found its way into the American culinary vocabulary. Jerk refers to the traditional Jamaican way of cooking pork, chicken, beef or seafood over a pit or on a grill, but it is the seasoning that makes it special. In Jamaica you can eat authentic jerk at jerk huts — casual roadside eateries where the meat is cooked outdoors over wood fires. But with this recipe for jerk rub, you can get true jerk flavor right in your home kitchen.

Makes about 1/2 cup

2 tablespoons dried minced onion
1 tablespoon onion powder
1 tablespoon granulated sugar
4 teaspoons ground thyme
2 teaspoons salt
2 teaspoons coarsely ground
    black pepper
2 teaspoons ground allspice
1 to 2 teaspoons cayenne
    pepper, to taste
1/2 teaspoon ground nutmeg
1/2 teaspoon ground cinnamon

In a small jar with a tight-fitting lid, combine onion, onion powder, sugar, thyme, salt, pepper, allspice, cayenne, nutmeg and cinnamon. Shake until seasonings are well mixed. Store seasoning mixture in a cool, dry place for up to a month.

To use: Rub seasoning mixture onto surface of ribs, beef, chicken, fish or vegetables. Or, lightly rub oil over meat, then sprinkle with seasoning mixture and pat onto surface. Grill as desired. Discard any excess seasoning mixture that has come in contact with raw meat.

Nearly 29 fewer people die in alcohol-related crashes every day since MADD began.

Mom's Barbecue Sauce

Sue Kurth
Food Editor, *Beloit Daily News*, Beloit, WI

My mom created this recipe, which I use often. It makes enough sauce to baste two cut-up chickens.

Makes about 1¹/₂ cups

1 cup cider vinegar	1 teaspoon dry mustard
¹/₂ cup ketchup	1 teaspoon garlic powder
2 tablespoons Worcestershire sauce	1 teaspoon salt
1 tablespoon granulated sugar	¹/₂ teaspoon hot pepper sauce

In a medium saucepan, combine vinegar, ketchup, Worcestershire sauce, sugar, dry mustard, garlic powder, salt and hot pepper sauce; mix well. Bring just to a boil; reduce heat and let simmer 10 minutes. Use immediately, or let cool and refrigerate, covered, for later use.

Use to baste chicken, ribs or other meats. Discard sauce after use.

Multi-Purpose Marinade

Beth W. Orenstein
Free-Lance Writer, Northampton, PA

I use this marinade for lamb, beef and turkey. The tougher the cut of meat, the longer it needs to marinate. It's a good idea to turn the meat occasionally while it's marinating.

Makes about 1¹/₄ cups

²/₃ cup vegetable oil or olive oil	¹/₂ teaspoon dry mustard
¹/₂ cup red wine vinegar	1 teaspoon granulated sugar
1 teaspoon salt	Dash hot pepper sauce

Combine oil, vinegar, salt, dry mustard, sugar and hot pepper sauce in a jar with a tight-fitting lid; shake to mix well. Refrigerate, covered, until needed.

Shake well before using to marinate lamb, beef, turkey or other meats. Discard marinade after use.

Mustard Steak Rub

Jane Baker
Free-Lance Writer, East Lansing, MI

It's possible to grill even in the winter in Michigan. The secret is wrapping the grill cover with several layers of heavy-duty aluminum foil and preheating the gas grill 15 to 20 minutes. For example, we grilled thick, juicy steaks for Christmas dinner, even though the temperature was below freezing and a light snow was falling. This mustardy rub, which makes enough to season about 2 pounds of steak, helps bring out the beef flavor.

Makes about 1/3 cup

3 tablespoons dry mustard
1 tablespoon coarsely ground
   black pepper

1 1/2 teaspoons garlic powder
1 teaspoon onion powder
1/2 teaspoon crushed red pepper

In a small mixing bowl, combine dry mustard, pepper, garlic powder, onion powder and red pepper flakes; mix well. Store in a tightly sealed container up to six months in the freezer.

To use: Coat steaks evenly with rub; refrigerate, covered, 1 to 2 hours before grilling. Discard excess rub that has been in contact with raw meat.

Oriental Lemon Marinade

Alice Handkins
Free-Lance Food Writer, Wichita, KS

This simple marinade adds an enticing flavor to chicken or pork. The sweet-tart taste of lemonade combines with soy sauce and spices to create a tantalizing flavor. Use thin slices of fresh lemon for garnish, or put lemon slices on the grill during the last few minutes of cooking and place a grilled lemon slice on top of each piece of chicken or pork. This recipe makes enough marinade for two cut-up chickens or 12 pork chops.

Makes about 2 cups

1 can (12 ounces) frozen lemonade concentrate, thawed, undiluted
2/3 cup soy sauce

2 teaspoons seasoned salt
1 teaspoon celery salt
1/4 teaspoon garlic powder

In a medium mixing bowl, combine lemonade concentrate, soy sauce, seasoned salt, celery salt and garlic powder; mix well. Refrigerate, covered, until needed.

To use. Place chicken pieces or pork chops in a shallow dish; pour marinade over meat. Refrigerate, covered, up to 24 hours; turn pieces occasionally. Remove meat from marinade, reserving marinade. Put marinade in saucepan and heat to boiling. Reduce heat and let marinade simmer until needed. Use heated marinade to baste meat during grilling. Discard remaining marinade.

Peach Salsa

Kasey Wilson
Food Columnist, *The Vancouver Courier*, Vancouver, BC, Canada

The tangy, sweet taste of this salsa goes great with salmon, spicy seafood, pork or chicken. You can vary the recipe by using nectarines or mangoes instead of peaches.

Makes about 1¹/₂ cups

4 peaches, peeled, pitted and
　finely chopped
2 jalapeño peppers, seeded and
　finely chopped
¹/₂ red bell pepper, finely chopped
1 clove garlic, minced

¹/₄ cup chopped fresh cilantro
2 tablespoons olive oil
2 tablespoons lime juice
Salt and freshly ground black
　pepper, to taste

In a medium mixing bowl, combine peaches, jalapeño peppers, bell pepper, garlic, cilantro, olive oil, lime juice, salt and pepper; gently mix. Refrigerate, covered, overnight to let flavors blend. Serve peach salsa with grilled salmon, poultry or meat.

There are an estimated 2.2 million alcohol-related crashes each year.

Shish Kebab Marinade

Janet Geissler
Food Editor, *Lansing State Journal*, Lansing, MI

I've never found another shish kebab marinade that I like as well as this one. The rosemary adds a delicate taste, while the citric acid in the lemon juice helps tenderize the meat. I like this with beef, but you also can use it with chicken or lamb. I alternate the beef cubes with mushrooms, onions and green bell peppers on the skewers, but feel free to try other combinations. This recipe makes enough marinade for about one pound of meat.

Makes about 3/4 cup

1/2 cup vegetable oil
1/4 cup lemon juice
1 clove garlic, minced

3/4 teaspoon salt
1/2 teaspoon dried rosemary
1/2 teaspoon black pepper

In a shallow dish, combine oil, lemon juice, garlic, salt, rosemary and pepper; mix well.

To use: Add 1 pound cubed beef, lamb or chicken to marinade; toss to evenly coat meat. Refrigerate, covered, overnight, turning meat occasionally. Remove meat from marinade; discard marinade. Thread meat and vegetables of choice onto 6 to 8 metal skewers. Grill as desired.

Strawberry-Mustard Brush

Narcisse S. Cadgène
Free-Lance Writer, New York, NY

This lively sweet-sour sauce will become as much a favorite in your household as it is in mine. Quick and easy to assemble, it complements poultry and pork especially well, but it's a nice change of pace for lamb or shrimp, too. I often take a jar as a hostess gift when I'm invited to a barbecue or swim party. This recipe makes enough sauce for about four servings of meat.

Makes 1/2 cup

1/4 cup strawberry jam
1/4 cup Dijon-style mustard
1 teaspoon coarsely ground
    black pepper

1/2 teaspoon dried rosemary or
    thyme (optional)

In a small saucepan or microwave-safe dish, combine jam, mustard, pepper and rosemary; mix well. Warm mixture on top of stove or in microwave oven. Stir well. Refrigerate, covered, until needed. Reheat and mix well before using.

To use: Generously brush sauce on chicken or pork during the last 10 minutes of grilling. This sauce scorches easily, so watch carefully and turn the meat as necessary. Discard remaining sauce.

About 36% of all fatally injured drivers were drunk at the time of the crash in 1993.

ACCOMPANIMENTS

136   Bean and Corn Salad

137   Big Bean Pot Beans

138   Broccoli-Cauliflower Salad

139   Chutney Broccoli Salad

140   Cilantro Garlic Bread

141   Confetti Cole Slaw

142   Couscous Salad

143   Cucumber Salad

144   Fruited Summer Slaw

145   German Potato Salad

146   Grown-Up S'Mores

147   Italian Bread Salad

148   Low-Fat Pasta Salad with Roasted Vegetables

149   Pick-Up Potato Salad

150   Sauerkraut Relish

150   Savory Corn Relish

151   Skewered Parmesan Garlic Bread

152   Southwest Macaroni Salad

153   World's Greatest Potato Salad

Bean and Corn Salad

Jim Hillibish
City Editor, *The Repository*, Canton, OH

Barbecued meats tend to be hot and spicy, so side dishes should complement those flavors by being on the bland side. This salad does its duty in a substantial, but not overwhelming, way. Served on a bed of lettuce, it's an excellent, low-calorie contrast to sizzling, grilled foods. This version is adapted from a collection of church picnic recipes from Canton, Ohio.

Makes 10 servings

1 can (16 ounces) kidney beans, drained
1 can (16 ounces) black beans, drained
1 can (10 ounces) whole-kernel corn, drained
1 green bell pepper, finely chopped
1 red bell pepper, finely chopped

3 tablespoons lime juice
2 tablespoons olive oil
2 tablespoons cider vinegar
Freshly ground black pepper, to taste
5 green onions, thinly sliced
2 tablespoons finely chopped fresh parsley

In a large serving bowl, combine kidney beans, black beans, corn, green and red bell peppers, lime juice, olive oil and vinegar; mix well. Refrigerate, covered, at least 2 hours to let flavors blend.

Just before serving, season salad with pepper. Garnish with green onions and parsley. Serve chilled.

More than 50% of all boating fatalities are alcohol-related.

Big Bean Pot Beans

Eleanor Ostman
Food Writer, *St. Paul Pioneer Press*, St. Paul, MN

> *My cousin, Betty Rostvold, is legendary for the cookouts and barbecues at her northern Minnesota lake home, next door to ours. She and her family think nothing of cooking for up to a hundred hungry people. She made these beans at a recent summer get-together.*

Makes 20 servings

1/2 pound bacon, chopped
2 1/2 cups chopped onions
1 can (15 or 16 ounces) kidney beans, drained
1 can (15 or 16 ounces) butter beans, drained
1 can (15 or 16 ounces) lima beans, drained

2 cans (21 ounces each) pork and beans, undrained
1/2 cup cider vinegar
1 teaspoon garlic powder
1 teaspoon dry mustard

In a large baking dish or Dutch oven, brown bacon and onions. Drain fat. Add kidney beans, butter beans, lima beans, pork and beans, vinegar, garlic powder and dry mustard; mix well. Bake in a preheated 350° oven 1 to 1 1/2 hours, or until beans are hot and bubbly. Let stand 20 minutes before serving.

Broccoli-Cauliflower Salad

Susan Manlin Katzman
Free-Lance Food Writer, St. Louis, MO

Back in the early '80s, when I was teaching cooking classes twice a week and writing a weekly food column, I was always on the lookout for recipes. "Try this one," my friend Elizabeth Hightower said. "It was my grandmother's and I think people will really like it." I tried it, liked it and taught it. Several years later, I adapted it for use by a supermarket chain's take-out department. The supermarket loved it and called it St. Louis Salad. When the chain opened a branch in Kansas City, the recipe became Kansas City Salad. By any name, it's the perfect barbecue side dish.

Makes about 6 servings

1 cup mayonnaise
1/4 cup crumbled cooked bacon
1/4 cup granulated sugar
1/3 cup grated Parmesan cheese
1/2 pound broccoli florets
   (about 3 cups)

1/2 pound cauliflower florets
   (about 3 cups)
1 small red onion, thinly sliced
Salt and black pepper, to taste

In a large mixing bowl, combine mayonnaise, bacon, sugar and Parmesan cheese; mix well. Add broccoli, cauliflower and onion; stir gently. Season with salt and pepper.

Refrigerate, covered, until ready to serve. Serve chilled.

1,746 people died in alcohol-related crashes from Thanksgiving to New Year's Eve in 1993.

Chutney Broccoli Salad

Eleanor Ostman
Food Writer, *St. Paul Pioneer Press*, St. Paul, MN

One of the delights of my job is talking to cooks at Minnesota's lakeside resorts. They know what makes guests happy and keeps them coming back. This recipe is based on one shared by the chef at Naniboujou Lodge on Minnesota's North Shore, edging Lake Superior. A huge hit with everyone who tastes it, this crisp, curry-flavored salad has become a standard for cookouts at our own lake home.

Makes 16 servings

2 heads broccoli, cut into bite-size pieces (florets and some stem)
1 1/2 pounds seedless red grapes (about 5 cups)
1/2 red onion, chopped
1 cup lightly toasted slivered almonds
2 cups mayonnaise
1 jar (9 ounces) chutney
2 tablespoons curry powder

In a large mixing bowl, combine broccoli, grapes, onion and almonds.

In a small mixing bowl, combine mayonnaise, chutney and curry powder; mix well. Stir mayonnaise mixture into broccoli mixture; mix well. Refrigerate, covered, until ready to serve. Serve chilled.

Cilantro Garlic Bread

Eleanor Ostman
Food Writer, *St. Paul Pioneer Press*, St. Paul, MN

I first tasted fresh cilantro on a visit to Southeast Asia in 1979, but several years went by before it was available in the supermarkets in the Twin Cities. Now it's everywhere — in stores and in recipes. Cilantro has a flavor that you either love or hate. I love it, and use it everywhere, even on grilled bread. This is a variation on a recipe from Chinese food expert Hugh Carpenter.

Makes 8 servings

1/2 cup butter or margarine	2 tablespoons chopped fresh chives
1/4 cup chili sauce	1/3 cup finely chopped fresh cilantro
1/4 teaspoon black pepper	1 loaf French bread, 12 inches long,
1/4 teaspoon cayenne pepper	unsliced
4 cloves garlic, minced	1/2 cup grated Parmesan cheese

In a small saucepan, combine butter, chili sauce, pepper, cayenne and garlic. Cook over low heat until butter bubbles around edge of pan. Remove from heat. Stir in chives and cilantro.

Split bread in half lengthwise. Brush each half generously with butter mixture. Sprinkle with cheese.

Toast bread on grill or under broiler until golden. Cut into slices to serve.

Nearly 54.6% of all traffic fatalities during Christmas were alcohol-related in 1993.

Confetti Cole Slaw

Beth W. Orenstein
Free-Lance Writer, Northampton, PA

Cole slaw is the perfect accompaniment to any barbecued main course. This recipe is quick and easy and worth the little extra effort for the homemade taste. Using a food processor to shred the cabbage and other vegetables makes preparation a snap.

Makes 8 to 10 servings

5 cups coarsely shredded cabbage (about 1 pound)
1 large tomato, seeded and finely chopped
1/2 cup chopped green bell pepper
1/2 cup sliced green onions
1/3 cup finely shredded carrots
1/2 cup lemon juice
1/2 cup granulated sugar
1/3 cup vegetable oil
1 teaspoon salt
1/2 teaspoon dry mustard

In a medium bowl, combine cabbage, tomato, bell pepper, green onions and carrots.

In a small saucepan, combine lemon juice, sugar, oil, salt and dry mustard; mix well. Bring to a boil. Pour hot dressing over cabbage mixture; toss to mix. Refrigerate, covered, 4 hours, or overnight, to let flavors blend. Serve chilled.

Couscous Salad

Susan Manlin Katzman
Free-Lance Food Writer, St. Louis, MO

Whenever the family gathers for a bring-a-dish barbecue, my daughter-in-law, Hilary Skirboll, wows us with her recipe for couscous salad. The dish has become a family mainstay not only because it is pretty, delicious and complements all barbecue entrées, but also because it receives high praise from the family vegetarian who thinks the dish was invented just for him. Not so. Hilary saw a similar recipe in a health food magazine and adapted the dish to suit her taste. It seems to suit everyone else's taste, too. Thank you, Hilary.

Makes 4 to 6 servings

2¼ cups water
1 medium carrot, finely chopped
1 medium zucchini, finely chopped
½ cup plus 1 tablespoon
   olive oil, divided
Pinch ground cinnamon
Pinch ground cloves
1½ cups quick-cooking
   couscous, uncooked

¼ cup white vinegar
2 tablespoons lemon juice
2 teaspoons Dijon-style mustard
1 clove garlic, minced
Salt and black pepper, to taste
½ cup raisins
½ cup toasted sliced or
   slivered almonds

Bring water to a boil in a large saucepan. Add carrot, zucchini, 1 tablespoon olive oil, cinnamon and cloves; boil 1 minute. Add couscous. Remove saucepan from heat; cover and set aside 5 minutes. Uncover and let couscous cool, fluffing often with two forks.

Combine vinegar, lemon juice, mustard, garlic and remaining ½ cup olive oil in a small bowl; mix well. Pour dressing over cooled couscous; toss lightly. Season with salt and pepper. Add raisins and almonds; toss to mix. Refrigerate, covered, until ready to serve. Serve chilled.

The red ribbon is a symbol of your pledge to be a sober driver.

Cucumber Salad

Susan Manlin Katzman
Free-Lance Food Writer, St. Louis, MO

The cliché tells us that cucumbers are cool. Well, according to my taste, you couldn't find any dish cooler (both literally and figuratively) to serve as an accompaniment to spicy barbecue. The hotter the barbecue, the cooler and more refreshing seem the cucumbers. But I love to serve this particular recipe at my own barbecues for another reason. The cucumbers have great flavor that marries exceedingly well with all grilled meats, but the dish contains no fat. Because the man I married views barbecues as the grand opportunity to indulge, I like to balance the menu with dishes he can take to heart (both literally and figuratively).

Makes 6 to 8 servings

4 large cucumbers	2 cups cold water
1 small red onion, thinly sliced	2 cups rice vinegar
1/3 cup chopped fresh mint	1 cup granulated sugar
1/3 cup chopped fresh cilantro	1 teaspoon salt
2 to 4 whole dried red chili peppers	

Score peel of each cucumber with tines of a fork. Cut off ends of each cucumber, cutting to beginning of seeds. Halve cucumbers lengthwise. With a spoon, scrape out and discard seeds. Cut each cucumber half into 1/4-inch-thick, half-moon-shaped slices.

Combine cucumbers, onion, mint, cilantro and chili peppers in a glass bowl. Put water, vinegar, sugar and salt in a mixing bowl; stir until sugar dissolves. Pour dressing over cucumber mixture; stir lightly. Refrigerate, covered, until ready to serve. Serve well chilled.

Fruited Summer Slaw

Debra Carr-Elsing
Food Writer, *The Capital Times*, Madison, WI

*When eating outside on a hot summer day, I like to have something cool
and refreshing on my plate. This fruited slaw is a family favorite. It's an
interesting combination of flavors and textures. The crispy crunch of
celery, cabbage and walnuts is balanced with the soft texture of
bananas and raisins. Folded throughout is a hint of tangy lemon juice.*

Makes 8 servings

1 can (8¼ ounces) pineapple
 chunks in syrup
1 carton (8 ounces)
 orange-flavored yogurt
1 tablespoon lemon juice
3 cups finely shredded cabbage
1 can (11 ounces) mandarin
 orange sections, drained

1 cup thinly sliced celery
¾ cup chopped walnuts
½ cup raisins
1 medium banana, peeled
 and sliced

Drain pineapple, reserving 2 tablespoons syrup. In a small bowl,
combine reserved 2 tablespoons pineapple syrup, yogurt and lemon
juice; mix well.

In a large bowl, combine drained pineapple, cabbage, mandarin
oranges, celery, walnuts and raisins. Fold yogurt dressing into
cabbage mixture. Gently fold in banana. Refrigerate, covered, until
ready to serve. Serve chilled.

Crashes involving men are more likely than those involving women to be alcohol- related.

German Potato Salad

Sue Kurth
Food Editor, *Beloit Daily News*, Beloit, WI

I've tried deli German potato salad many, many times, and I've always been disappointed when I compare its taste to the wonderful flavor of my homemade recipe. Nothing compares to this version, which isn't as acidic as some commercial ones. The mild sweet-sour taste shares the stage with bacon and sour cream. It's a nice change from regular potato salad at summer picnics, and it is good served hot or cold.

Makes 4 to 6 servings

9 medium-size red potatoes, peeled
Salted water
1/2 pound bacon
2 hard-cooked eggs, peeled
    and chopped (optional)
1 medium onion, chopped
    (optional)

2 tablespoons all-purpose flour
3/4 cup granulated sugar
1/2 cup cider vinegar
1/3 cup water
1 cup sour cream

In a large saucepan, cover potatoes with salted water; boil until tender. Drain potatoes and let cool slightly. Cut cooked potatoes into bite-size pieces; put in a large mixing bowl.

In a large skillet, cook bacon until crisp. Remove from pan and drain on paper towels. Crumble bacon; add to potatoes. If desired, add hard-cooked eggs and onion; mix gently.

Drain off all but 2 tablespoons bacon drippings. Add flour; mix well. Add sugar, vinegar and water; mix well. Cook over low heat, stirring almost constantly, until mixture is smooth and thick. Remove from heat; stir in sour cream.

Pour sour cream dressing over potato mixture; mix gently. Serve warm or chilled.

Grown-Up S'Mores

Barbara Yost
Feature Writer, *The Phoenix Gazette*, Phoenix, AZ

This is the adult version of the Girl Scout favorite. We loved them then, so why give them up just because we grew up? The basics are the same. Just add a little flavoring to make a not-too-sweet finish for a summer barbecue.

Makes 1 serving

2 marshmallows
1 milk chocolate candy bar
2 graham crackers

$1/2$ teaspoon ground cinnamon
$1/2$ teaspoon instant espresso
   powder

For each S'More, thread 2 marshmallows on long metal skewer or pointed stick. Hold over low heat of gas grill or low coals of charcoal grill or wood fire. Toast 2 to 3 minutes, or until golden, turning often.

Place unwrapped candy bar on graham cracker; sprinkle with cinnamon and espresso powder. Top with toasted marshmallows and second graham cracker. Press sandwich lightly to spread marshmallow layer evenly.

Repeat to make as many S'Mores as needed. Yum!

Alcohol involvement is highest for men age 21-30.

Italian Bread Salad

Constance Hay
Free-Lance Food Writer, Columbia, MD

Italian Bread Salad is a refreshing side dish for hot weather dining, as well as a clever way to use leftover bread. Fresh ripe tomatoes are a natural summer ingredient; during the winter I often substitute a jar of roasted peppers. This recipe offers an opportunity to use your family's favorite vegetables and be creative.

Makes 4 servings

4 cups cubed Italian, French or any crusty bread

2 tomatoes, finely chopped

1/2 cup chopped green bell pepper

1/2 cup finely chopped celery

1/2 to 1 cup chopped cooked beef, chicken or turkey (optional)

2 tablespoons thinly sliced fresh basil leaves

1/3 cup olive oil

2 tablespoons balsamic vinegar

1 clove garlic, minced

1/2 teaspoon fennel seeds

Salt and black pepper, to taste

Put bread cubes on an ungreased baking sheet. Toast in a preheated 350° oven 10 minutes. Let cool.

In a large bowl, combine toasted bread cubes, tomatoes, bell pepper, celery, beef and basil; toss to combine.

In a small bowl, combine olive oil, vinegar, garlic, fennel seeds, salt and pepper; mix well. Pour dressing over salad; toss thoroughly. Let salad absorb dressing for about 10 minutes before serving.

Note: One-half cup bottled Italian salad dressing can be substituted for the oil, vinegar, garlic, fennel seeds, salt and pepper. One jar (7 1/4 ounces) roasted peppers, drained, can be substituted for tomatoes.

Low-Fat Pasta Salad with Roasted Vegetables

Nancy Ross Ryan
Food Editor, *Restaurants & Institutions*, Des Plaines, IL

Everyone loves pasta salads, but anyone who knows the calorie and fat content of the usual pasta salad indulges with guilt. In this recipe, low-fat marinara sauce is used in place of mayonnaise or oil-based vinaigrette. (At the supermarket, look for marinara sauces that specify low fat and have about 40 calories per 1/2 cup.) This can be served at room temperature or chilled, making it a convenient make-ahead dish. Serve it as a side dish or in larger portions as a vegetarian main dish.

Makes 12 servings

1 pound fusilli (spiral) or rotelle (cartwheel) pasta, uncooked

2 medium-size yellow onions, cut into eighths (about 1 cup)

2 to 3 small gold- or red-skinned potatoes, cut into eighths (about 1 cup)

1 cup sliced carrots (1/4-inch slices)

1 cup cut green beans (1-inch lengths)

1 cup sliced zucchini (1/2-inch slices)

1 red bell pepper, coarsely chopped (about 1 cup)

Salt and freshly ground black pepper, to taste

1 can (15 ounces) garbanzo beans, drained and rinsed

1 cup shredded mozzarella cheese

1/3 cup grated Parmesan or Romano cheese

2 cups low-fat marinara sauce (homemade or bottled)

Cook pasta al dente according to package directions. Drain in a colander, then let cold water run over pasta to cool it; drain well.

Spray two 15x10x1-inch baking pans or two 14-inch pizza pans with nonstick cooking spray. Spread onions, potatoes, carrots, green beans, zucchini and bell pepper evenly in prepared pans. Lightly spray vegetables with nonstick cooking spray. Season vegetables with salt and pepper. Roast, uncovered, in preheated 400° oven 30 minutes, or until vegetables are tender and lightly brown. To prevent charring, loosely cover with aluminum foil during last 10 minutes.

In large mixing bowl, combine drained pasta, roasted vegetables, garbanzo beans, mozzarella cheese, Parmesan cheese and marinara sauce. Toss to mix thoroughly.

Serve at room temperature, or refrigerate, covered, and serve cold.

Remember that all forms of alcoholic beverages are drugs.

Pick-Up Potato Salad

Carolyn Flournoy
Food Columnist, *The Times*, Shreveport, LA

Being a food columnist means never being able to say, "I'm sorry," when asked to bring a dish for a cookout. But I have devised a no-brainer potato salad "recipe" that is always one of the hits of any get-together. Everyone asks for the recipe. I usually mumble, "Oh, it's just something I whipped up at the last minute." And I'm not telling an untruth. I picked up the main ingredient on my way home from work.

Makes 6 to 8 servings

1 quart store-bought deli
    potato salad
4 hard-cooked eggs, divided
1 1/2 teaspoons celery seeds
2 teaspoons Dijon-style mustard

2 tablespoons finely chopped
    fresh parsley
1 teaspoon seasoned pepper
Paprika

Transfer potato salad to a serving bowl. Peel and coarsely chop 3 hard-cooked eggs. Add chopped eggs, celery seeds, mustard, parsley and seasoned pepper to potato salad; mix well. Smooth down top of potato salad; wipe off rim and edge of bowl. Peel and slice remaining hard-cooked egg; arrange slices on top of salad. Sprinkle with paprika. Refrigerate, covered, until serving time. Serve chilled.

Sauerkraut Relish

Jane Gray
Food Editor, *Ludington Daily News*, Ludington, MI

> *When I first heard about this dish I was skeptical, but once I tried it, I was sold. Its tartness is a perfect accent to grilled meats, poultry and fish.*

Makes 4 to 6 servings

2 cups sauerkraut, rinsed, drained
 and cut into short lengths
1/2 cup chopped green bell pepper
1/4 cup pimento strips
1/2 cup mayonnaise

1 tablespoon prepared
 horseradish
1 teaspoon Worcestershire sauce
1/2 teaspoon salt
1/8 teaspoon black pepper

In a medium mixing bowl, combine sauerkraut, bell pepper, pimento, mayonnaise, horseradish, Worcestershire sauce, salt and pepper; mix well. Refrigerate, covered, until ready to serve.

Savory Corn Relish

Janet Geissler
Food Editor, *Lansing State Journal*, Lansing, MI

> *Here's a delicious, easy salad that is a nice change-of-pace from cole slaw or potato salad.*

Makes 8 servings

2 can (12 ounces each)
 whole-kernel corn, drained
1 cup coarsely chopped
 green bell pepper
1 cup finely chopped celery
1/2 cup chopped onion
1 jar (2 ounces) diced
 pimentos, drained

2/3 cup vegetable oil
1/4 cup plus 2 tablespoons
 white vinegar
2 teaspoons salt
1/2 teaspoon black pepper
11/2 teaspoons dry mustard

In a large mixing bowl, combine corn, bell pepper, celery, onion, pimentos, oil, vinegar, salt, pepper and dry mustard; mix well. Refrigerate, covered, to let flavors blend. Serve chilled.

Most persons are impaired by alcohol before they are legally intoxicated.

Skewered Parmesan Garlic Bread

Ann Corell Wells
Food Editor, *The Grand Rapids Press*, Grand Rapids, MI

Garlic bread is a must with grilled meats. This recipe is one of my family's favorites, especially for summer meals at our Lake Michigan cottage, where I like to cook everything on the grill. We often have two charcoal grills going to accommodate the meat and side dishes.

Makes 6 to 8 servings

1 loaf (16 ounces) French or Italian bread, unsliced
1/2 cup margarine or butter, softened

2 cloves garlic, minced (or to taste)
1/4 cup freshly grated Parmesan cheese

Cut bread into 2- to 3-inch cubes with a serrated knife. In a small bowl, combine margarine, garlic and Parmesan cheese; mix well. Spread mixture on all sides of bread cubes. (Recipe can be prepared to this point, then place bread cubes on a baking sheet and refrigerate until time to cook.)

If using bamboo or wooden skewers, soak them in water for 30 minutes to prevent burning.

Thread bread cubes on metal or bamboo skewers. Place skewers on gas grill over medium heat or on charcoal grill 4 to 6 inches from medium coals. Cook 5 to 10 minutes, or until golden brown, turning frequently. Serve hot.

Southwest Macaroni Salad

Jane Baker
Free-Lance Writer, East Lansing, MI

I prepared this recipe often when I lived in Arizona as an accompaniment to grilled chicken, meat or fish. It's also great to take to potluck suppers. When I moved to Michigan, I discovered that this salad was just as good here as in Arizona, so I continue to prepare it often. I personally prefer macaroni salad to potato salad for outdoor meals and particularly like the spicy tang of this recipe.

Makes 10 to 12 servings

1 pound elbow or shell macaroni, uncooked
1 can (12 ounces) whole-kernel corn, drained
1 can (4 ounces) chopped green chilies, drained
1 medium cucumber, finely chopped
1 small onion, finely chopped

3/4 cup red wine vinegar
1/4 cup olive oil
1 teaspoon dried basil
1 teaspoon dried thyme
1/2 teaspoon dried oregano
1/8 teaspoon hot pepper sauce
Salt and black pepper, to taste
1/2 cup mayonnaise

Cook macaroni according to package directions. Drain in colander, then let cold water run over pasta to cool it; drain well.

In a large mixing bowl, combine macaroni, corn, chilies, cucumber and onion; mix well. Add vinegar, olive oil, basil, thyme, oregano, hot pepper sauce, salt and pepper; mix well. Refrigerate, covered, 8 hours, or overnight. Stir in mayonnaise just before serving. Serve chilled.

A person's ability to drive is affected at blood alcohol content levels as low as .02.

World's Greatest Potato Salad

Eleanor Ostman
Food Writer, St. *Paul Pioneer Press*, St. Paul, MN

My mother, one of the world's great cooks, taught me to make potato salad this way. After she died, I wrote down specifics for the recipe in my head. The secret is marinating warm potato slices.

Makes 12 to 15 servings

5 pounds potatoes
1/2 cup vegetable oil
1/4 cup white wine vinegar
1 teaspoon dry mustard
   (or more, to taste)
1 tablespoon granulated sugar
1 teaspoon paprika
1 teaspoon salt
Freshly ground black pepper,
   to taste
6 green onions, sliced

1 large sweet onion, finely chopped
3 cups mayonnaise-type
   salad dressing
1/4 cup heavy or light cream
1 to 2 tablespoons Dijon-style
   mustard, to taste
8 hard-cooked eggs, divided
6 ribs celery, finely chopped
Lettuce leaves
Paprika, for garnish

Cook unpeeled potatoes in water to cover in a large stockpot. While potatoes are cooking, combine oil, vinegar, dry mustard, sugar, 1 teaspoon paprika, salt and several generous grindings of pepper; beat with a wire whisk until well blended.

When the potatoes are tender but not mushy, remove from heat and drain. Peel them as soon as possible, while they are still very warm. Chop potatoes into a large bowl or a 15x10x1-inch jelly-roll pan. As soon as a layer of potatoes has been chopped, sprinkle with some green onions and sweet onion and drizzle with some marinade. Repeat layers of potatoes, green onions, sweet onion and marinade until all are used. Refrigerate, covered, several hours, or until thoroughly chilled.

When ready to mix salad, combine salad dressing, cream and mustard; taste and add more mustard, if desired. Peel and chop 7 of the hard-cooked eggs. Add chopped eggs and celery to potatoes. Add salad dressing mixture; stir until potatoes are coated. Spoon potato salad into a lettuce-lined bowl. Peel and slice remaining hard-cooked egg. Garnish salad with egg slices and paprika. Serve at once.

Cold showers, coffee, or fresh air won't sober up a drunk — only time will help.

INDEX

A

Almonds
Chutney Broccoli Salad, 139
Couscous Salad, 142
Fish Coating, 124

Anchovies
Mahi-Mahi with Caesar Sauce, 81

Apple Juice
Chicken on the Grill, 52
Chicken Tenders in Tangy
   Mustard Sauce, 53

Apples
Grilled Apples, 97
Grilled Leg of Lamb, 26
Maple Apple Rings, 108

Apricots
Curried Fruit Glaze, 122
Fire-and-Ice Kebabs, 94

B

Bacon
Bacon-Wrapped Shrimp, 70
Big Bean Pot Beans, 137
Broccoli-Cauliflower Salad, 138
Chili Relleno Chicken, 54
German Potato Salad, 145
Kiwi Venison Steaks, 30
Mahi-Mahi in Ti Leaves, 80
Mexican Chicken, 63

Bananas
Fire-and-Ice Kebabs, 94
Fruited Summer Slaw, 144
Grilled Sundaes, 99

Beans
Bean and Corn Salad, 136
Big Bean Pot Beans, 137
Low-Fat Pasta Salad with
   Roasted Vegetables, 148

Beef
Beef Fajitas, 18
Flank Steak Appetizer, 20
Garlic Steak Sandwiches, 22
Great Balls of Fire, 23
Italian Bread Salad, 147
Manhattan Steak, 33
Reubenburgers, 37
Seasoned Steak with
   Grilled Peppers, 38
Sour Cream Beef Burgers, 39
Spiedini Sandwiches, 41
The Perfect Burger, 44
Tulsa Kebabs, 45
Zesty Flank Steak, 46

Bell Peppers
Bean and Corn Salad, 136
Confetti Cole Slaw, 141
Greek-Style Kebabs, 57
Grilled Pepper Sunburst, 102
Herbed Vegetables on Skewers, 106
Italian Bread Salad, 147
Marinated Tofu and
   Vegetable Brochettes, 109
Mussels with Curry Butter, 82
Peach Salsa, 132
Sauerkraut Relish, 150
Savory Corn Relish, 150
Seafood Boats, 84
Seafood-Citrus Kebabs, 85
Seasoned Steak with
   Grilled Peppers, 38

Blackberries
Blackberry Cobbler, 93

Bologna
Okie Dokie Barbecued Bologna, 35

Bouillon Cubes
Grilled Vidalia Onions, 105

Bread
Cilantro Garlic Bread, 140
Grilled Quail on Toast, 56
Italian Bread Salad, 147
Oyster Pan Roast, 83
Skewered Parmesan Garlic Bread, 151

Bread Crumbs
Sour Cream Beef Burgers, 39
Zesty Italian Tomatoes, 114

Broccoli
Broccoli-Cauliflower Salad, 138
Chutney Broccoli Salad, 139

Brown Sugar
Chuckwagon Rub, 119
Fire-and-Ice Kebabs, 94
Great Grilled Tofu, 96
Grilled Ham, 24
Grilled Pineapple with
    Brown Sugar Sauce, 103
Lamb Steaks Supreme, 31
Midwest-Style Spareribs, 34
Seafood Boats, 84
Texas-Style Ribs, 43

Butter
Compound Butters, 120
Lemon-Herb Chicken Breasts, 61

Buttermilk
Buttermilk Marinades, 117

C

Cabbage
Confetti Cole Slaw, 141
Fruited Summer Slaw, 144

Capers
Grilled Caponata, 98
Hot Dogs — Your Way, 28

Carrots
Confetti Cole Slaw, 141
Couscous Salad, 142
Hot Dogs — Your Way, 28
Low-Fat Pasta Salad with
    Roasted Vegetables, 148

Cauliflower
Broccoli-Cauliflower Salad, 138

Celery
Fruited Summer Slaw, 144
Italian Bread Salad, 147
Savory Corn Relish, 150
The Perfect Burger, 44
World's Greatest Potato Salad, 153

Cheese
Barbecued Pizza, 49
Broccoli-Cauliflower Salad, 138
Chili Relleno Chicken, 54
Cilantro Garlic Bread, 140
Fish Coating, 124
Grilled Pepper Sunburst, 102
Grilled Polenta or Grits, 104
Hot Dogs — Your Way, 28
Hot Potatoes, 107
Low-Fat Pasta Salad with
    Roasted Vegetables, 148
Reubenburgers, 37
Skewered Parmesan Garlic
    Bread, 151
Turkey Burgers, 67

Chicken
Barbecued Chicken Wings, 48
Barbecued Pizza, 49
Chicken Kebabs Bombay, 50
Chicken Nugget Sandwiches, 51
Chicken on the Grill, 52
Chicken Tenders in Tangy
    Mustard Sauce, 53
Chili Relleno Chicken, 54
Cilantro Grilled Chicken Breast, 55
Greek-Style Kebabs, 57
Herbed Chicken Breasts, 58
Honey-Mustard Chicken, 59
Italian Bread Salad, 147

Kebabs with Jalapeño-Honey Sauce, 60
Lemon-Herb Chicken Breasts, 61
Lemony Herb Chicken, 62
Mexican Chicken, 63
Mushroom-Stuffed Chicken Thighs, 64
Mustard Barbecued Chicken, 65
Spicy Lemon Chicken, 66

Chili Peppers
Cincinnati Dry Rub, 118
Mexican Chicken, 63

Chili Sauce
Chili Shrimp, 72
Cilantro Garlic Bread, 140

Chocolate
Grown-Up S'Mores, 146

Chutney
Chutney Broccoli Salad, 139
Grilled Leg of Lamb, 26

Cilantro
Cilantro Garlic Bread, 140
Cucumber Salad, 143

Cloves
Compound Butters, 120
Grilled Peaches, 101

Coconut
Fire-and-Ice Kebabs, 94
Grilled Fruit Sundaes, 99

Coffee
Grown-Up S'Mores, 146
Lamb Steaks Supreme, 31

Corn
Bean and Corn Salad, 136
Fresh Vegetable Kebabs, 95
Michigan-Style Corn-on-the Cob, 110
Savory Corn Relish, 150
Southwest Macaroni Salad, 152

Couscous
Couscous Salad, 142

Cucumbers
Cucumber Salad, 143
Cucumber Sauce, 121
Southwest Macaroni Salad, 152

D

Dill
Compound Butters, 120

E

Endives
Super Grilled Salad, 113

Eggplant
Grilled Caponata, 98
Herbed Vegetables on Skewers, 106

Eggs
German Potato Salad, 145
Ham Burgers, 27
Pick-Up Potato Salad, 149
The Perfect Burger, 44
World's Greatest Potato Salad, 153

F

Fish
California-Style Fish in
    Lettuce Wraps, 71
Grilled Fish Sandwich, 75
Grilled Fish with Herbs, 74
Grilled Salmon, 76
Halibut with Thyme, 77
Hawaiian Grilled Swordfish with
    Papaya, 78
Mahi-Mahi in Ti Leaves, 80
Mahi-Mahi with Caesar Sauce, 81
Snappy Snapper, 86
Swordfish on the Grill, 88
Tarragon Grilled Salmon, 90

G

Garlic
Barbecued Chicken Wings, 48
Beef Fajitas, 18
Buttermilk Marinades, 117
California-Style Fish in
    Lettuce Wraps, 71

Chuckwagon Rub, 119
Cilantro Grilled Chicken Breast, 55
Flank Steak Appetizer, 20
Garlic Steak Sandwiches, 22
Great Grilled Tofu, 96
Grilled Green Onions, 100
Grilled Leg of Lamb, 26
Grilled Salmon, 76
Halibut with Thyme, 77
Herb-Garlic Rub, 126
Manhattan Steak, 33
Mussels with Curry Butter, 82
Peach Salsa, 132
Shish Kebab Marinade, 133
Skewered Parmesan Garlic
    Bread, 151
South African Safari Kebabs, 40
Swordfish on the Grill, 88
Zesty Flank Steak, 46

Graham Crackers
Grown-Up S'Mores, 146

Grapefruit
Seafood-Citrus Kebabs, 85

Grapes
Chutney Broccoli Salad, 139

Grits
Grilled Polenta or Grits, 104

H

Ham
Grilled Ham, 24
Ham Burgers, 27

Honey
Honey-Mustard Chicken, 59
Honey-Mustard Glaze, 127
Mustard Barbecued Chicken, 65
St. Louis Pork Steaks, 42

Hot Dogs
Foiled Franks, 21
Hot Dogs — Your Way, 28

I

Ice Cream
Blackberry Cobbler, 93
Grilled Fruit Sundaes, 99

J

Jalapeño
Chili Relleno Chicken, 54
Great Balls of Fire, 23
Kebabs with Jalapeño-Honey
    Sauce, 60
Peach Salsa, 132

Jam
Strawberry-Mustard Brush, 134

Kiwifruit
Kiwi Venison Steaks, 30

L

Lamb
Grilled Lamb Kebabs, 25
Grilled Leg of Lamb, 26
Lamb Steaks Supreme, 31

Lemons
Boating Pork Chops, 19
Chicken Nugget Sandwiches, 51
Cilantro Grilled Chicken Breast, 55
Clams and Mussels in their Shells, 73
Grilled Fish with Herbs, 74
Lemon-Herb Chicken Breasts, 61
Lemon-Herb Rabbit, 32
Lemony Herb Chicken, 62
Mahi-Mahi with Caesar Sauce, 81
Plum Delicious Ribs, 36
Spicy Lemon Chicken, 66

Lemon Juice
Confetti Cole Slaw, 141
Dad's Smoking Sauce, 123
Oriental Lemon Marinade, 131
Shish Kebab Marinade, 133

Limes
Baked Sweet Potatoes, 92

Chicken Tenders in Tangy
  Mustard Sauce, 53
Mussels with Curry Butter, 82
Virgin Islands Grilled Turkey, 68

M

Marmalade
Grilled Apples, 97
Ham Burgers, 27

Marshmallows
Grown-Up S'Mores, 146

Mayonnaise
Broccoli-Cauliflower Salad, 138
Chutney Broccoli Salad, 139
Cucumber Sauce, 121
Grilled Fish Sandwich, 75
Herbed Chicken Breasts, 58
Sauerkraut Relish, 150
Snappy Snapper, 86
Softshell Crabs on the Grill, 87
Southwest Macaroni Salad, 152

Mint
Cucumber Salad, 143
Grilled Lamb Kebabs, 25
Herbed Chicken Breasts, 58

Molasses
Midwest-Style Spareribs, 34
Okie Dokie Barbecued Bologna, 35

Mushrooms
Grilled Lamb Kebabs, 25
Herbed Vegetables on Skewers, 106
Hot Potatoes, 107
Marinated Tofu and
  Vegetable Brochettes, 109
Mushroom-Stuffed Chicken Thighs, 64
Seafood-Citrus Kebabs, 85
Tulsa Kebabs, 45

Mustard
Chicken Tenders in Tangy
  Mustard Sauce, 53
Curried Fruit Glaze, 122
Midwest-Style Spareribs, 34
Mom's Barbecue Sauce, 129

Multi-Purpose Marinade, 129
Mustard Barbecued Chicken, 65
Mustard Steak Rub, 130
Snappy Snapper, 86
Strawberry-Mustard Brush, 134
World's Greatest Potato Salad, 153
Zesty Flank Steak, 46

O

Olives
Grilled Caponata, 98
Grilled Pepper Sunburst, 102
Hot Dogs — Your Way, 28

Onions
Apple-Tarragon Marinade, 116
Bacon-Wrapped Shrimp, 70
Barbecued Chicken Wings, 48
Beef Fajitas, 18
Big Bean Pot Beans, 137
Broccoli-Cauliflower Salad, 138
Foiled Franks, 21
Fresh Vegetable Kebabs, 95
Garlic Steak Sandwiches, 22
Grilled Green Onions, 100
Grilled Lamb Kebabs, 25
Grilled Vidalia Onions, 105
Halibut with Thyme, 77
Herbed Vegetables on Skewers, 106
Hot Potatoes, 107
Jamaican-Style Jerk Rub, 128
Lemon-Dill Scallops, 79
Low-Fat Pasta Salad with
  Roasted Vegetables, 148
Manhattan Steak, 33
Mushroom-Stuffed Chicken Thighs, 64
New Potatoes on a Stick, 111
Onion Lollipops, 112
Plum Delicious Ribs, 36
Sour Cream Beef Burgers, 39
Spiedini Sandwiches, 41
Super Grilled Salad, 113
Texas-Style Ribs, 43
The Perfect Burger, 44
Turkey Burgers, 67
World's Greatest Potato Salad, 153

Oranges
California-Style Fish in
  Lettuce Wraps, 71
Fire-and-Ice Kebabs, 94
Fruited Summer Slaw, 144
Grilled Ham, 24
Seafood-Citrus Kebabs, 85

P

Papaya
Hawaiian Grilled Swordfish with
  Papaya, 78

Parsley
Chili Shrimp, 72
Herb-Garlic Rub, 126
Mussels with Curry Butter, 82

Pasta
Low-Fat Pasta Salad with
  Roasted Vegetables, 148
Southwest Macaroni Salad, 152

Peaches
Grilled Peaches, 101
Peach Salsa, 132

Peanut Butter
Virgin Islands Grilled Turkey, 68

Peppercorns
Cincinnati Dry Rub, 118

Pimentos
Sauerkraut Relish, 150
Savory Corn Relish, 150

Pineapples
Fire-and-Ice Kebabs, 94
Fruited Summer Slaw, 144
Grilled Fruit Sundaes, 99
Grilled Pineapple with
  Brown Sugar Sauce, 103
Hawaiian Grilled Swordfish with
  Papaya, 78
Healthful Marinade, 127
Seafood Boats, 84
Tangy Grilled Shrimp, 89

Plums
Plum Delicious Ribs, 36

Pork
Boating Pork Chops, 19
St. Louis Pork Steaks, 42
Texas-Style Ribs, 43

Potatoes
German Potato Salad, 145
Hot Potatoes, 107
Low-Fat Pasta Salad with
  Roasted Vegetables, 148
New Potatoes on a Stick, 111
Pick-Up Potato Salad, 149
World's Greatest Potato Salad, 153

Q-R

Quail
Grilled Quail on Toast, 56

Rabbit
Lemon-Herb Rabbit, 32

Raisins
Couscous Salad, 142
Fruited Summer Slaw, 144
Maple Apple Rings, 108

Rice
Seafood Boats, 84

S

Sauerkraut
Hot Dogs — Your Way, 28
Reubenburgers, 37
Sauerkraut Relish, 150

Shallots
Tarragon Grilled Salmon, 90

Shell Fish
Bacon-Wrapped Shrimp, 70
Chili Shrimp, 72
Clams and Mussels in their Shells, 73
Lemon-Dill Scallops, 79
Mussels with Curry Butter, 82
Oyster Pan Roast, 83
Seafood Boats, 84
Seafood-Citrus Kebabs, 85
Softshell Crabs on the Grill, 87

Tangy Grilled Shrimp, 89

Sour Cream
Cucumber Sauce, 121
German Potato Salad, 145
Kebabs with Jalapeño-Honey Sauce, 60

Soy Sauce
Dad's Smoking Sauce, 123
Flank Steak Appetizer, 20
Fresh Tuna Marinade, 125
Great Grilled Tofu, 96
Grilled Salmon, 76
Oriental Lemon Marinade, 131
Texas-Style Ribs, 43
Tulsa Kebabs, 45
Virgin Islands Grilled Turkey, 68

Spareribs
Midwest-Style Spareribs, 34
Plum Delicious Ribs, 36

Squash
Herbed Vegetables on Skewers, 106

Sweet Potatoes
Baked Sweet Potatoes, 92

T

Teriyaki Sauce
Healthful Marinade, 127

Ti Leaves
Mahi-Mahi in Ti Leaves, 80

Tofu
Great Grilled Tofu, 96
Marinated Tofu and
    Vegetable Brochettes, 109

Tomatoes
Chicken Nugget Sandwiches, 51
Confetti Cole Slaw, 141
Grilled Caponata, 98
Grilled Lamb Kebabs, 25
Italian Bread Salad, 147
Lemon-Dill Scallops, 79
Super Grilled Salad, 113
The Perfect Burger, 44
Tulsa Kebabs, 45
Zesty Italian Tomatoes, 114

Tortillas
Beef Fajitas, 18

Turkey
Italian Bread Salad, 147
Turkey Burgers, 67
Virgin Islands Grilled Turkey, 68

V

Venison
Kiwi Venison Steaks, 30
South African Safari Kebabs, 40

Vinegar
Apple-Tarragon Marinade, 116
Big Bean Pot Beans, 137
Cucumber Salad, 143
Fresh Tuna Marinade, 125
Mom's Barbecue Sauce, 129
Multi-Purpose Marinade, 129
Southwest Macaroni Salad, 152
World's Greatest Potato Salad, 153

W

Walnuts
Fruited Summer Slaw, 144
Grilled Apples, 97
Maple Apple Rings, 108

Z

Zucchini
Couscous Salad, 142
Fresh Vegetable Kebabs, 95
Low-Fat Pasta Salad with
    Roasted Vegetables, 148
Marinated Tofu and
    Vegetable Brochettes, 109
Tulsa Kebabs, 45

Y

Yogurt
Fruited Summer Slaw, 144